Polish - Lithuanian Regiments
1717 - 1794
Gembarzewski's Regiments

By
Vincent W. Rospond

Images by
Bronislaw Gembrazewski

T0325211

Polish - Lithuanian Regiments 1717 - 1794: Gembarzewski's Regiments
By Vincent W. Rospond
Cover by Bronislaw Gembarzewski
This edition published in 2022

Winged Hussar is an imprint of

Winged Hussar Publishing, LLC
1525 Hulse Rd, Unit 1
Point Pleasant, NJ 08742

Copyright © Winged Hussar Publishing
ISBN 978-0-988953-26-0

LCN 2022940423

Bibliographical References and Index
1. History. 2. Poland. 3. 18th Century

Winged Hussar Publishing, LLC All rights reserved
For more information
visit us at www.wingedhussarpublishing.com

Twitter: WingHusPubLLC
Facebook: Winged Hussar Publishing LLC

This book is sold subject to the condition that it shall not, by way of trade or otherwise, be lent, resold, hired out, or otherwise circulated without the publisher's prior consent in any form of binding or cover other than that in which it is published and without a similar condition, including this condition, being imposed on the subsequent purchaser.

The scanning, uploading, and distribution of this book via the Internet or via any other means without the permission of the publisher is illegal and punishable by law. Please purchase only authorized electronic editions, and do not participate in or encourage electronic piracy of copyrighted materials. Your support of the author's and publisher's rights is appreciated. Karma, its everywhere.

Table of Contents

Preface

One of the challenges on researching the Polish-Lithuanian Army of the eighteenth century is that the partitioning powers sought to erase the name Poland from history as if it never existed. Two world wars and time have helped in this effort, but the dedication of historians and individuals throughout the world have brought a significant body of informationto light..

At the start of the eighteenth century Poland-Lithuania looked like it was one of the biggest powers in Eastern Europe. They had just fought a series of successful wars against the Turks, in alliance with the major western European powers as part of the Holy League in the 1680's - 90's. The next elected king in 1797 dynastically aligned the Commonwealth with Saxony and made peace with Muscovy. The Great Northern War, starting in 1700 changed all that as the invading Swedes made short work of the Saxons and pushed deep into Russia. By the time the Great Northern War ended, Poland had become a Russian Protectorate. Despite what has often been portrayed a slow decline in the early part of the century, the state made attempts to reform itself. It moved away from a feudal military structure and organized their military along western lines, which included permanent regiments and command and control. The second part of the century was a very dynamic time in the development of the country, warfare and the European Revolutionary wars of the 1790s. The time of the partitions featured two generals that influenced the American Revolution, the first written constitution in Europe and the development of military tactics that were felt into the nineteenth century.

Unless otherwise indicated drawings are by Bronislaw Gembarzewski. Here are abbreviations used for other sources:

MWPW - Polish Army Museum	JH - Jozef Harasimowicz
AO - Aleksander Orlowski	MS - Michal Stachowicz
JPN - Jan Piotr Norblin	VR - Vincent Rospond
GNR - Gabriele Nicholas Raspe	

I. Introduction

The Polish - Lithuanian Army (also known as "the Commonwealth" and for ease in this book referred to as "Poland" or "Polish") was a major power in East-Central Europe for over 300 years. The Commonwealth consisted of a Union of two nations – Poland (referred to as "The Crown") and the Grand Duchy of Lithuanian (referred to as "The Duchy"). The Election of the Saxon kings was originally thought of as a way to strengthen the state. By the start of the 18th century, however, internal squabbles reduced her to the status of client state.

The outbreak of the Great Northern War was initially looked on as an opportunity to take revenge on the old enemy – The Swedes, while allying with the Saxons and Muscovites in the field. The war was an unmitigated disaster for the Commonwealth. From the end of the Great Northern War (1717) until the end of the first partition the Poles for the most part only fought each other. Following the Great Northern War, Commonwealth's army was limited in size to 24,000 troops and Russia was a guarantor of her security which meant it had a free reign to interfere in the country's internal policy. Prussia became a partner in this Russian policy and used Poland for men, material and resources.

Internal and external politics of the period kept the Saxon Dukes on the throne as the acceptable candidate to all parties. The Saxon Kings wanted the position but were accepted as long as they did not interfere with the internal policies. In those cases when a stronger nationalist candidate came to power (Stanislaw Leszczyński) the neighboring powers strove to return the Saxon dynasty to the throne. If a group of nobles believed the King /Grand Duke was acting contrary to law, they could form a "confederation" which in most cases would lead to armed conflict. Several Confederation were formed during this period which aided the Nations were descending into.

At the death of August III, Tsarina Catherine II pushed for her former lover Stanisław Poniatowski to be elected King over Augustus' son. Poniatowski was a son of a noble clan, well connected, but not a power player in Polish politics. The new King was a child of the Enlightenment who wished to raise his country up from its declining fortunes. In the process of initiating reforms and through interference of the Russian court a group of traditionalist nobles formed a confederation in the town of Bar which gave the Confederation its name. The Barists believed they were defending their freedoms against the King. This in turn initiated a civil war that spread throughout the country and lead to the first partition of Poland.

Following the first partition the Polish-Lithuanian Commonwealth sought to reform itself. A series of legislative efforts results in the first written constitution outside of the United Sates and the creation of the Commonwealth of two nations which united Poland-Lithuania as one entity. This in turn forced the Poles to defend their Constitution against the Russians that resulted in the second partition. In an effort to save what they could of their nation Tadeusz Kosciuszko led an uprising against the Russians, was defeated in 1794 resulting in the disappearance of Poland from the map until its rebirth in the aftermath of World War I.

Kings of Poland 1700 – 1795

(Left) August II (Jan Matejko). (Right) Stanislaw Leszczynski (Pesne)

Augustus II (The Strong) – House of Wettin 1697 – 1704 (deposed) / 1706 (abdicated)

Stanisław I – Leszczyński 1705 – 1709 (deposed)

Augustus II (The Strong) – House of Wettin 1709 – 1733

Stanisław I Leszczyński 1733 – 1734 (deposed) /1736 (abdicated)

Augustus III – House of Wettin 1734 – 1763

Stanisław Augustus Poniatowski 1764 - 1795

(Left) Augustus III (Jan Matejko). (Right) Stanislaw Augustus Poniatowski (Jan Matejko)

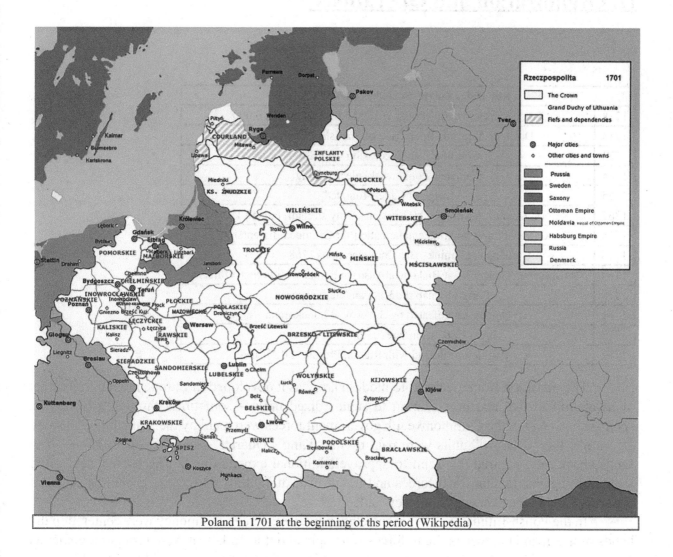

Poland in 1701 at the beginning of ths period (Wikipedia)

II. Organization and Operations

Key Dates for the Period 1718 – 1772	
1718	Russian Protectorate – Polish Army 18,000, Lithuania 6,000
1733	Death of Augustus II, election of Stanisław Leszczynski
1733	War of Polish Succession till 1736
1764	Stanislaw Poniatowski elected King
1765	Corps of Cadets founded
1767	Reform Senators kidnapped by Russian/ Army strength falls to 12,000
1768	Cardinal Laws granting emancipation for Orthodox dissenters
1768	Uprising in Ukraine / Bar Confederation (1768 – 1772)
1769	Barists set up Generality at Biała near Austrian border with French Officers
1770	Barists kidnap the King and he escapes
1771	Dumouriez defeated by Suvorov at Lanckorona
1772	Jasna Góra capitulates ending Bar activity
1772	First Partition of Poland with Russia, Prussia and Austria

The transition from medieval to modern army as it developed in Europe moved from units of indetermined size and organization to standardized units – sometimes through government sponsorship. Within the Commonwealth government forces were paid by the Sejm although some forces like the "Landowi" units were paid by the "King's Quarter" from the royal estates. Any funds above that required the Sejm to approve additional expenditures. The nobles were often suspicious against raising royal forces and the growth of centralized power despite the fact that Poland's borders faced enemies on every side.

In the Polish-Lithuanian Commonwelath power, resources and money were centered in the hands of the great landowners. State forces were spread out to forts that were brought together as needed to meet demands. These were supplemented with forces raised and paid for by noble families. Independent cavalry companies were called chorągiew (khor-ogi-ev) which we loosely translate into "Companies". Several companies might be combined into a pułk, (poowk) or regiment. Throughout this period state infantry regiments were made up of understrengthed battalions and companies. The head of the regiment was the Chief and operational command was the Colonel. Prior to 1772, many of the regular units had officers and ranks on leave at any one time. This led to a small army having an even more diminished force which relied on magnate[1] armies to keep help order.

The Crown (Poland) and Duchy (Grand Duchy of Lithuanian) armies operated independently of each other but were organized as mirror images. In theory the overall commander of the Commonwealth forces in each kingdom was a Grand Hetman who was appointed by the King. The Grand Hetman was assisted by the Field Hetman, who had operational control of

---

[1]Magnates were large landowners who accumulated large personal fortunes and controlled political life.

10

armies. The powers of the Hetman were curtailed during some of the initial reforms. Divisions and brigades were not established but organized as the situation dictated under the command of a Major General. The King nominally controlled the Guard, which consisted of a regiment of infantry and cavalry in both the Crown and the Duchy.

The artillery was under the command of its own general with batteries disbursed throughout the Commonwealth in fortresses and as well as being integrated within infantry regiments. They were primarily bronze guns made before 1732 that range from 24 to 1.5 lbs.

Following the defeat in the Great Northern War and reorganization under Russia protection, the Polish Infantry began to adopt a western organization while the cavalry retained an "Eastern Europe-

Augustus II at the Battle of Kalisz, 1706 (unknown)

an" flavor. The Saxon kings tried to institute a more formal army structure, but the nobles resisted those changes out of fear of absolutism and the stage was set to curtail Poland-Lithuania's military.

Rather than numbered, the infantry regiments were named for their commanders and followed the Saxon organization which consisted of two battalions numbering sixteen companies with:

Staff

2 Colonels (one of which was the Proprietor or inhaber)	1 Adjutant
1 Lieutenant Colonel	1 Auditor
2 Majors	1 Chaplin
1 Quartermaster	1 Carpenter
1 Regimental barber/doctor	1 Captain -Lieutenant

Battalions

11 Captains	
15 Lieutenants	16 Senior Sergeants
5 Second Lieutenants	16 Sergeants
16 Ensigns (1 color per bataillon)	16 Sergeant Fouriers
64 Corporals	8 Medical assistants
128 Grenadiers	32 Drummers
	1,024 Privates

Totaling 1,391 men

(Left) A captain (Rotmistrz) of Hussars from 1740. (Right) Towarzysz of Hussars 1746. (Center) Towarzysz of Hussars 1749

Following the defeat in the Great Northern War, Cavalry and Dragoon Regiments began to be organized along more traditional manners - organized with four squadrons consisting of eight companies. Each company comprising twelve officers and seventy-five men with an additional staff of fifteen men, providing a total of seven hundred eleven men.

Hussar banners were organized around companies called, *rotas*, which were comprised around *Towarzysz* and *Pocztowy*. In the time of armored Hussars, the Towarzysz (literally "Comrades") was the nobleman and the *Pocztowy*, his retainers. By the mid-18th century the *Towarzysz* were armed with lances in the front rank and the Pocztowy followed up with sabres and firearms.

Units were raised and stationed in each of the districts: Wielkopolska, Malopolska, Ukraine, Podolski and Wolynski. Between 1733 - 1735 the cavalry consisted of banners of Hussars, Pancerni and Light. In 1717 the Guard Infantry was made up of two twelve company battalions and one eight company battalion totaling 2,330 men. From 1745 - 63 it numbered 1,500 men

In 1765 infantry regiments were organized into two battalions. Each battalion had a grenadier and five musketeer companies. In addition, each regiment had an artillery company of four light guns. Grenadier and fusilier regiments had two battalions of six companies.

In the Crown lands cavalry consisted of sixteen banners of hussars (heavy cavalry). There were seventy-six banners of pancerni (medium cavalry), fourteen banners of light cavalry and seven regiments of dragoons.

The Grand Duchy of Lithuania cavalry had six banners of hussars, twenty-five banners of medium cavalry (also known as petyhorst), twelve banners of Tartars, eight banners of Cossacks and four regiments of dragoons.

Magnate Armies

While growing in importance throughout the 17th century, by the 18th century the largest military formations in some areas of the country were controlled by the great Magnate families such as Opaliński, Lubomirski, Potocki, Ossoliński, Zamoyski, Koniecpolski, Sieniawski, Czartoryski, Sapieha, Chodkiewicz, Pac and Radziwiłł's. They were able to uniform, equip and supply units of infantry, artillery and of course cavalry. These units mirrored the organization of regular army units or modeled them on Austrian or Prussian units. The Radziwiłł's had the largest army during the middle part of the century with 2-3 thousand men, organized in infantry, artillery and dragoons units and professionally trained by foreign officers.

Most often they were uniformed in liveried colors of the families and were sometimes used to keep order. By the time of King Stanislaw Poniatowski, the magnates were convinced to given up their private forces so that men and material could find their way back into the state coffers.

The War of Polish Succession

The War of Polish Succession was the only "declared" action Polish forces fought between the Great Northern War and the Bar Revolt. The meager Polish state forces fought for the elected Monarch, Stanislaw Leszczynski and the "foreign" choice of Augustus III. The majority of the war was fought outside of Poland, but several engagements were fought across the country, including a siege at Gdansk.

The Seven Years War

Although the Commonwealth did not directly participate in the Seven Years War, armies crossed their territories to attack each other. Several magnates took individual units into service for one side or the other.

Stanislaus Leszczyński by Adam Manyoki. ***Stanisław Leszczyński*** (1677 – 1766) was elected king of Poland-Lithuania and ruled from 1704-1709, during the Great Northern War, and again from 1733-1736 during the War of Polish Succession. In the later he was elected in an open election, but Russia favored the Austrian candidate Frederick Augustus III of Saxony and invaded the country to force the issue. He was forced to flee to France where he rules over an area of Lorraine

The Bar Confederation 1768 - 1772

There was no central organization for the Barist. The insurrection was actually a series of small confederations, each with their own organization and goals. Additionally, each believed it was superior to the others. Because most participants had some martial experience they were generally organized in companies under a captain. They lacked a coordinated grand strategy, but initially they consisted of hit and run cavalry action backed up by infantry units. As foreign "experts" came to advise the rebels, they began to abandon mobile warfare in favour of capturing cities to act as a base. This required assistance from technical experts to make use of artillery and required even more troops to garrison these cities. Because many of the soldiers came from the existing organization of the Polish Army, they would have used that as a basis for organizing their companies. The Barists maintained some popular support based on the vague ideas of expelling foreign influence and "Catholic" principals, which allowed them to capture large areas of the country from royal troops, but as Russian and Austrian troops moved in and cut off supplies from the French and Ottomans, they were overwhelmed.

Hussars in cuirassies in 1732 based on Mock, Brass helmet with white plume, Crimson collar with gold trim. Penants are white and yellow.

Trumpeters of the Hussars, based on porcelin figures. Pocztowy of the hussars, 1746.

Pocztowy of Light Cavalry 1746 - 1750

Infantry from the time of Augustus II

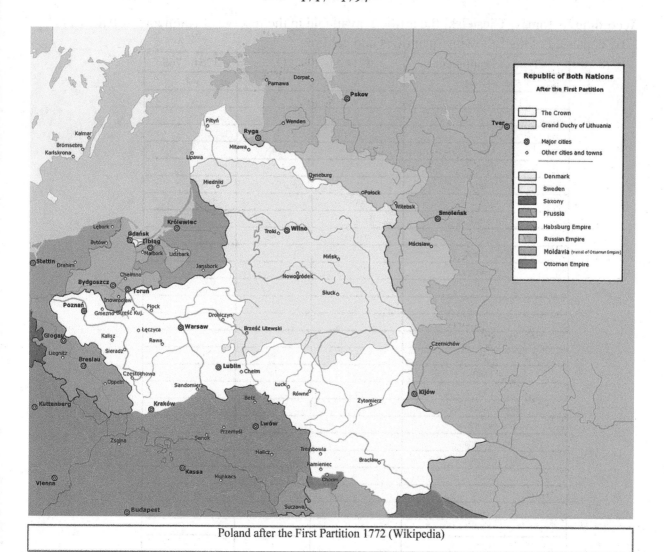

Poland after the First Partition 1772 (Wikipedia)

According to Tomasz Ciesielski the artillery available in the reserve at Kamients between 1718 - 1765 consisted of the following quantities and calibres.

Type of Equipment	1718	1733	1751-1765
Bronze Cannons			64
24 lbs	4	4	-
12 lbs	3	3	-
6 lbs	24	25	-
5 lbs	6	6	-
4 lbs	5	7	-
3 lbs	5	11	-
2 lbs	3	4	-
1.5 lbs	3	-	-
.75 lbs	1	-	-
Iron Cannons			43
24 lbs	6	6	-
8 lbs	-	1	-
6 lbs	11	13	-
4 lbs	-	2	-
3 lbs	8	9	-
2.5 lbs	4	-	-
2 lbs	2	11	-
1 lbs	-	1	-
Bronze swivel 3 lbs	1	1	1
Iron swivel 2 lbs	10	10	10
Bronze mortars			
60 lbs	1	-	-
50 lbs	-	1	-
16 lbs	1	-	-
15 lbs	2	2	-
12 lbs	1	-	-
10 lbs	-	1	-
9 lbs	-	1	-
6 lbs	-	2	-
2 lbs (hand grenade mortars)	6	7	8
Iron mortars			
125 lbs	1	1	-
35 lbs	2	-	-
32 lbs	-	2	-
24 lbs	1	1	-
20 lbs	-	1	-
16 lbs	2	-	-
15 lbs	4	2	-
14 lbs	-	4	-
12 lbs	-	1	-
3 lbs	12	11	-
Iron hand mortars frmae in wood	3	2	2
Hooked muskets (heavy wall muskets)	245	187	205

1772 - 1791

Key Dates for the Period 1772 – 1791	
1775	Permanent Council abolishes private armies
1776	Cavalry organized into National Cavalry Brigades
1782	Buying of ranks is abolished
1788	Great Sejm authorizes the army at 100,000 men
1788	Army reformed to join Russia against the Ottomans, but Catherine rejects the offer
1789	King authorizes three Major Generals – Prince Louis of Wurttemberg, Józef Poniatowski and Thaddeus Kosciuszko
1790	Treaty of alliance with Prussia
1791	May 3rd Constitution / The name "Commonwealth" is replaced in documents with "The State"
1791	Prussia and Austria accept the Constitution and the rules of succession

Regiments were known by the names of their commanders, but numbering started to be used. It was around this time that the first army manuals were developed and started to stress national obligations. Their organizational structure remained the same as it was prior to the first partition. In the 1770's the crown army was formed into four administrative divisions: Wielkopolska, Malopolska, Wolyńsko-Podolska and Ukraińska. In Lithuania there was just the administrative district of Vilnius. Both armies had artillery, engineers and pontoniers in a separate administrative unit known as "equipment".

Infantry regiments abandoned the tricorne hat and turnback coat for a shako and jacket in 1788. Some historians have speculated that the units adopted uniforms based on the Russian model in the hopes they would fight with them against the Ottomans, but nothing came of this. These changes, led the way to the reforms of the May Constitution.

By 1776 the cavalry was organized into National Cavalry Brigades. In 1784 National Cavalry brigades consisted of twenty-four squads of 144 troopers. The Guard cavalry had eight squads of 47 troopers. Cavalry was equipped with a pair of pistols, swords, lance and short musket - dragoons also had a bayonet. As part of the new rules instituted in 1785, the kontusz (pronounced kon-toosh) was shortened to a jacket that became the traditional lancer jacket (kurtka).

During this period an artillery train was organized under the army, rather than civilian control. The artillery was re-organized with cannon based on Austrian design and by 1779 it was organized again on the French Gribeauvale system. Artillery began to be cast by the Crown for the first time in 80 years and thru 1789 yielded guns in various calibers for field use. In addition, guns were privately cast for regimental use. The calibers used were 24, 12, 6, 5, 4, 3, 2 and 1.5 lbs. There were also 6 and 8-inch howitzers for use in the field and as well as a variety of mortars. The equipment was painted red as was the custom of the Saxon army.

Crown Infantry in 1776. GNR

The Royal Guard in summer uniforms as part of a painting by Canaletto in the 1770's.

National Cavalry in the 1770's. GNR

Polish Officer in the 1770's. GNR

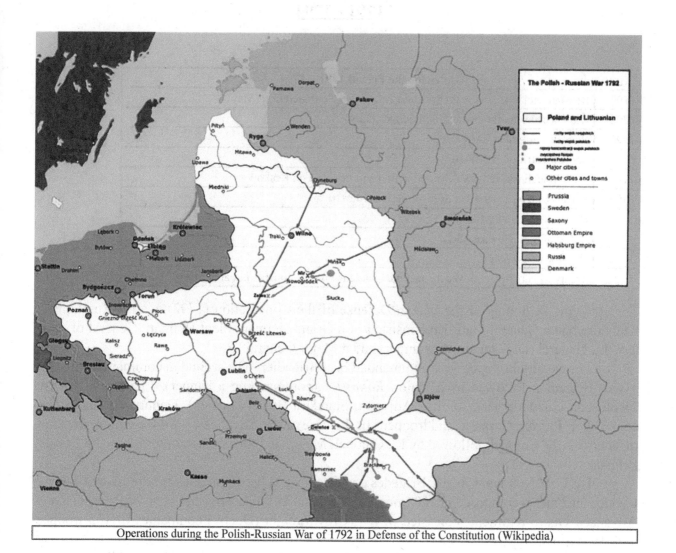

Operations during the Polish-Russian War of 1792 in Defense of the Constitution (Wikipedia)

1791 - 1794

Key Dates for the Period 1791 – 1794	
1792	Russian declaration of war (Apr) and Targowica Confederation (May)
1792	King accedes to Targowica Confederates (July)
1792	Warsaw surrenders (Aug)
1793	Second Partition is ratified
1794	Gen. Madaliński refuses de-mobilization and marches on Krakow
1794	Kosciuszko issues the Act of Insurrection (March)
1794	Battle of Racławice (Apr)
1794	Battle of Maciejowice (Oct)
1794	Warsaw Falls (Nov)
1795	Treaty of Partition removes the last independence of the Polish-Lithuanian Republic

At the beginning of the War in Defense of the Constitution (1792) against Russia, each Kingdom had a General Staff that consisted of a Grand Hetman, Field Hetman, General of Artillery, Lt. General (Divisional Commander) and a Major General.

The cavalry brigades were commanded by a Brigadier. The second in command was called a Vice-Brigadier, followed by a Major, *Rotmister* (commanding a banner), Lieutenant, Second Lieutenant, Quartermaster, Auditor, Adjutant, Standard Bearer (Ensign), Deputy, Comrade, Sargent Major, Furrier, Corporal and trooper. In the case of the Advance Guard Regiment, the commander was the Colonel, followed by Lt. Colonel, Major, and then rank structure as in the Cavalry Brigade.

By 1792 National Cavalry Brigades consisted of twelve companies for the Crown and sixteen for the Duchy, composed of 150 troopers, with a staff of nineteen and twenty-one respectively. Advanced Guard regiments consisted of ten (Crown)/eight (Duchy) companies of 135 troopers with 19 staffers.

In infantry regiments the nominal head was titled the Colonel-in-Chief, while the operational leader was the Colonel, followed by Lt. Colonel, Major, Captain (head of the Company), Auditor, Regimental Quartermaster, Adjutant, Lieutenant, Second Lieutenant, Standard Bearer (Ensign), Cadet Officer, Warrant Officer, Sargent, Furrier, Corporal and soldier.

Infantry regiments consisted of three battalions totaling twelve companies, each company consisting of 176 soldiers. Additional independent companies include, the Grand Hetman's Hungarian Company had 73 soldiers, the Field Hetman's Hungarian company had 73 soldiers and the rifle corps consisted of four battalions, each of four companies, each company had a stated strength of 147 soldiers.

The Artillery was commanded by a Major General of the Artillery, followed by Regimental Colonel and Lt. Colonel. Operationally, the artillery was dispersed by company and batteries usually based in fortresses until needed in the field. The operational command would then start with a Major, followed by a Captain, Quartermaster, Adjutant, Lieutenant, 2nd Lieutenant, Artificer, Staff Furrier, Commissary, Furrier, Master Gunner and Gunner.

Each infantry regiment had an artillery battery (4 guns) of men attached to it. Soldiers were designated from the ranks of the regiment to serve 2 to 3 pounders battalion guns. By 1792 artillery batteries consisted of 12lb and 6 lb batteries and 6-inch howitzers. The guns were made of iron and bronze with iron bands on the carriages. Guns were towed by wagons. By May 1792 there was the preliminary organization of some artillery into horse artillery units along the Prussian model. Gembarzewski shows horse artillery gunners from the horse guard regiment in 1794. At this point, the equipment was painted green which mimicked closer to Russian custom.

For Engineers and Pontoniers the head was the Chief of the Corps, followed by the Colonel, Lt Colonel, Captain, Lieutenant, 2nd Lieutenant, Conductor, Unter-Officer, Miner and Sapper.

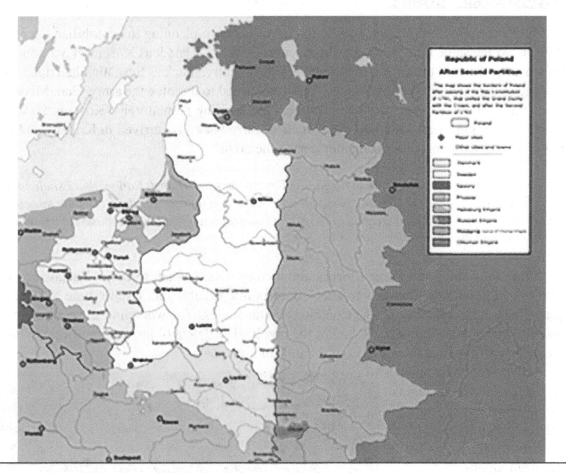

Poland-Lithuania after the Second Partition and Prior to the Kosciuszko Uprising (Wikipedia)

The War in Defence of the Constitution

During the period of the Long Sejm (1788-1792) while Russia was occupied in a war with the Ottomans, the Commonwealth attempted to reform itself, instituting a series of reforms which culminated in the 3rd of May Constitution in 1791. This was the first adopted written constitution in Europe, but it was not looked upon favorably by the partitioning powers. Although Prussia had agreed to a defensive treaty with the Commonwealth, they encouraged Russia to put down the Constitution. The Russians invaded leading to a series of engagements in the remaining eastern portion of the country. At the same time Catherine used a favorite Russian tactic and encouraged a group of nobles to swear a Confederation at Targowice stating that the Constitution violated the noble prerogatives; thus giving the Russians a legal pretense to invade. The King saw continued fighting as futile despite the urgings of his military commanders and surrendered to the Confederates. A truce was declared where units remained in place while a final peace was negotiated. This peace resulted in the Second Partition in 1793.

The Kosciuszko Uprising

While the army sat idle, the partitioning powers began planning to demobilize the remaining forces. At the same time, several military commanders – Thaddeus Kosciuszko among them – planned an uprising in the hope of winning back the country, much as the nation had done during the Deluge of the mid-17th century. As the Russians pushed to dissolve the army, Gen. Madalinski rode his troops out of his encampment and started the uprising prematurely. Kosciuszko was out of the country trying to gain aid, and was forced to hurry back. He arrived in Krakow and on 24 March 1794 and swore an oath as Dictator during the crisis:

> *I, Tadeusz Kościuszko, hereby swear in the face of God to the whole Polish Nation, that I shall not use the power entrusted to me for anyone's personal oppression, but only for the defence of the integrity of the borders, for retaking the sovereignty of the Nation, and for strengthening the universal freedom. So help me God and the innocent Passion of His Son!*

From there he lead his small forces to a victory over Russian forces at Racławice. Prussia also joined in with the Russians to attack the Commonwealth and despite some victories, the weight of the invaders wore down the Commonwealths forces. The wounding and capture of Kosciuszko at Maciejowice hastened the end of the revolt. The defeat of the Commonwealth's forces led to the 3rd Partition and the removal of Poland from the map.

After an abortive attempt to start a revolt out of Ottoman territory, Polish volunteers began arriving in France and Italy leading to the formation of the first Polish Legions.

The Constitution Of The 3rd May 1791 by Jan Matejko

Soldiers of 1794. Riflemen of the 10th regiment, a soldier in the foot guards and national cavalry troopers. AO

Pocztowy of the National Cavalry attacking Russian Infantry. AO

The Polish encampment showing National Cavalry, Militia Cavalry and infantry, regular infantry of the Wodzicki Regiment and an officer of the Advanced Guard. MS

Prince Jozef Poniatowski as commander of the Guards with Guard Infantry to the left.

III. Field Operations

The War of Polish Succession

The War of Polish Succession grew out of the dynastic struggles across multiple monarchies that were all put in motion at one time. In the Great Northern War, Stanisław Leszczyński was elected King under Swedish auspices in 1704 and removed in 1709 with the fall of Swedish fortunes forcing Stanisław to flee to France. Stanisław's daughter Maria, eventually married Louis XV in 1725. Upon Stanisław's removal, Augustus II was returned to the throne. In 1717 the traditional funding of the army through the "King's Quarter" was eliminated and taxes specifically earmarked for the army was passed in the Sejm.

When Augustus II died in 1733, he had not secured the succession of his son Augustus and the throne of Poland-Lithuania was considered up for grabs. In 1732 Austria, Prussia and Russia signed a secret treaty called The Treaty of Three Black Eagles to oppose the election of Stanisław and Augustus III, in favor of Manuel of Portugal. France used its influence to convince some of the great families such as the Potocki's and Czartoryski's to support the candidacy of Lezczyński. The convocation Sejm passed a resolution that excluded Manuel of Portugal and Augustus III in March 1733. Despite this Augustus negotiated concessions with Austria and Russia for their support to his election. These included giving up Polish claims to Livonia, Russian consent over the ruler of Courland and recognition of Maria Theresa's son to the Hapsburg throne.

In August 1733, a Russian Army under Field Marshal Peter Lacy took thirty thousand troops into Poland-Lithuanian to exert influence over a meeting of the Sejm. Despite this, in September the Sejm elected Stanisław Lezczyński ruler of the Commonwealth. A minority of electors then moved across the Vistula under the protection of the Russian forces to elect Augustus III. Despite the illegality of the election, Russia and Austria recognized Augustus as King, while France recognized Stanisław. This initiated a period of fighting across Europe that lasted until 1738.

The Russians, commanded by Peter Lacy, quickly captured the capital city of Warsaw

and installed Augustus as potential heir, forcing Stanislaus to flee to Gdańsk, where he was besieged for some time by a Russian-Saxon army that came under the overall command of Field Marshal Burkhard Christoph von Münnich. Danzig capitulated in June 1734, and Stanislaus was forced to flee once more, this time first to the city of Königsberg and eventually to France. This ended major military activity in Poland itself, although it continued to be occupied by foreign troops as Augustus dealt with partisan supporters of Stanislaus. A group of nobles and aristocrats supporting Stanislaus

Adam Tarło was the Starosta of Jasło and the commander of partisans of the short-lived Dzików Confederation. He was killed by Count Kazimierz Poniatowski in a duel in 1744

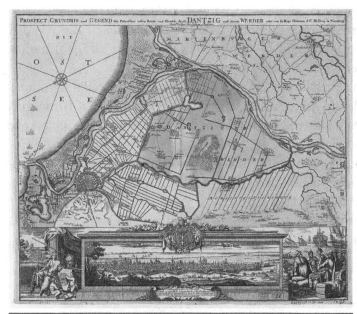

Operations around the seige of Danzig (Gdansk)

formed the Confederation of Dzików in late 1734, and under their commander, Adam Tarło, tried to fight the Russian and Saxon troops, but their efforts were ineffective. In 1734 battles were fought at Wyszecin and Miechów with varying success, but in the end, Russian, Saxon and Prussian interference prevailed over troops in support of Stanislaw.

The ***Battle of Miechów*** was fought on April 13, 1734 by armies of Stanisław Leszczyński under the command of Adam Tarło, against Saxon forces. It was one of the few victories of the Poles over the Saxons and the Russians in the war years of 1733 – 1735.

The ***Battle of Wyszecin***, also known as the Battle of Wyszeczyn, took place on 20 April 1734 during the Polish War of Succession. The crown army, commanded by the Lublin voivode, Adam Tarło, fought a battle with the Russian army of General Piotr Lacy near the village of Wyszecin.

The commander Adam Tarło, was trying to link up with the French who were supposed to land in the vicinity of Puck, headed with his unit in that direction. Tarło's forces were estimated at 8,000 cavalry but it was probably less. According to the voivode of Lublin he had 130 regiment militia, 2 regiments of the regular cavalry and 400 dragoons. After joining with the remnants of the troops from the castellan of Czersk, Kazimierz Franciszek Rudziński, who had been scattered near Świecie, when he came across a corps of 3,000 soldiers near Tuchola Russian troops commanded by Generals Biron and Zagrażski. Despite the numerical superiority, Tarło assessed the combat value of his forces as low and entered into negotiations. In view of the great numerical advantage of his opponent, Zagrażski agreed to enter into talks and send Tarło adjutant to Gdańsk. At the same time, the commander-in-chief of the army besieging Gdańsk, Field Marshal Burkhard Christoph Münnich, sent General Lacy to help Zagrażski with 5,000 troops not used when besieging the city, cavalry and cannons.

Learning about the enemy's approach, Tarło took up position south of Wyszecin with his flank turned to the south, in the direction of Piotr Lacy. The Cossacks came in the front line, with three companies of horse grenadiers, followed by four regiments of dragoons on horseback on the

The Seige of Danzig

25

left wing and 2 composite regiments of dragoons on the left wing. Two dragoon regiments were on horseback and in reserve. When Lacy arrived, the Russians unexpectedly attacked Tarło's army near Wyszecin on 20 April. The Polish forces managed to organize his forces into battle formation, but despite fierce resistance, his troops were pushed back due to inferior training.

The fleet fell into the hands of the Russians, who paid for their victory with significant losses. Shortly thereafter, another Confederate defeat at **Puck** at the hands of General Biron took place, which led to the expulsion of the Polish forces from Pomerania and allowed the Saxon and Russian armies to continue the siege of Gdańsk.

In what became known as the Pacification Sejm, held in June–July 1736, Augustus was confirmed as king of Poland and Grand Duke of Lithuania. This also reinforced the Russian control over Polish-Lithuanian foreign policy and military.

In 1734 and 1750 the army was involved in operations against uprisings on the frontier by Cossacks (**Haidamak Uprisings**). In 1744 there was a Civil War in Poland where government troops nominally fought for the Crown.

The Encampment of the Saxon-Polish Army from the 1730's by Jan Mock
A detail from the above, below

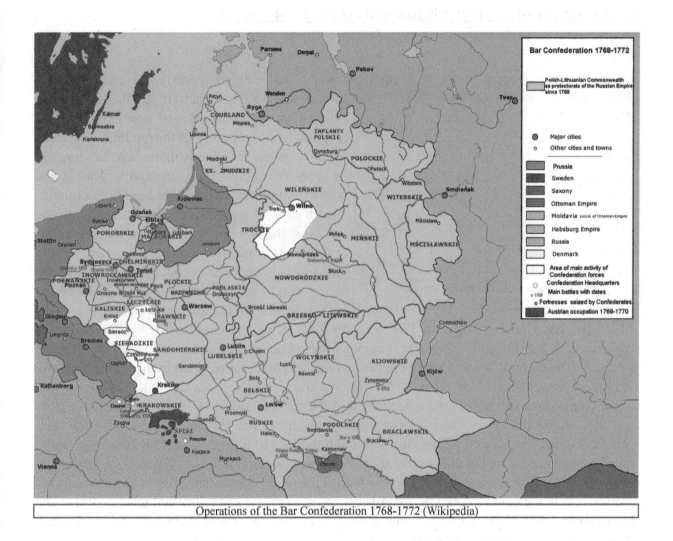

Operations of the Bar Confederation 1768-1772 (Wikipedia)

Operations of the Polish-Lithuanian Army 1764 – 1772

Camp of haidamakas by Juliusz Kossak

The reign of Stanislaw Augustus Poniatowski saw increased activity of the diminished Polish-Lithuanian armies and saw an attempt to reclaim the former glory of the republic. The early troubles began with the Koliyivshchyna Uprising in 1768-69 which was encouraged by Russia and who eventually were forced to help the Commonwealth's forces put down the outbreak. One of the leaders in the rebellion was Ivan Gonta, commander of Count Franciszek Potocki's Cossack Militia unit from Uman. The engagemnent of Commonwealth forces on the eastern frontier allowed the Bar Confederation to gain momentum.

The Bar Uprising began in 1768 as a result of perceived concessions by Poniatowski's government to Russia and Prussia over religious liberties but was rooted in continued interference in the government by Russia. There were various factions that played a part in the momentum and subsequent exploitation of issues in the Commonwealth. The King was trying to establish a way for the Commonwealth to become independent of Russia and was forced to send Polish troops to fight the Confederation after trying to negotiate with them. The Barists associated Poniatowski with the Tsarina and viewed all his efforts through the lens of a puppet ruler. Russia both found ways to create instability but did not like the revolutionary nature of the Confederation – in the end helped to defeat it. France and Austria provided aid the rebels – for France it was a way to support its adherents in the Commonwealth; for Austria a way to create instability and gain territory. The Barists gained control of vast areas of the country but could never hold them for long. In the end, when they kidnapped and supposedly tried to have the King killed, they lost support and momentum. In the end this resulted in the first Partition of Poland.

Fighting during the Bar Uprising ebbed and flowed across the Commonwealth. At different times the rebels were able to cross the Borders south and west, only to re-appear in other areas. What is interesting is that battle sites for the Bar Uprising were often revisited by Polish troops

Polish-Cossack skirmish during Bar Confederation by Waclaw Pawiszak.

in their fights against the Russians in 1792 and 1794.

The **Battle of Słonim** was fought on July 12, 1769 during the early stages of Confederation of Bar where Confederate troops led by Kazimierz Pulaski met up with and withdrew before the Russian forces of the *Wachmeister* to the right bank of Shchara, destroying the bridge in the process. The Cossacks of the Wachmeister forced the ford across the river and repaired the bridge. The remaining Russian troops crossed the bridge and organized themselves in their usual formation, i.e. infantry in the center and the cavalry on wings.

Karol Stanisław Radziwiłł (1734 - 1790) by Konstanty Aleksandrowicz

The Confederates opposed the Russians with most of their forces, but placed part of the cavalry behind the grove as an ambush. While leading the attack, the Russians set their left wing in a position convenient for the attack by the Polish unit hidden in the forest - the attack of this unit crushed the cavalry of the Russian left wing. The right Russian wing was also defeated. As a result of this situation the isolated Russian infantry, though not attacked by the Poles, withdrew from the battlefield.

The **Battle of Białystok**, also known as the **Battle of Olmont** - the battle fought on July 13, 1769 between the troops of the Bar Confederates and the Russian army. The Bar forces were under the command of Józef Bierzyński and Kazimierz Pułaski with about 4,000 troops - volunteers and deserters from the regular army with 18 cannons. Russian forces under the command of Aleksander Golitsyn had about 800 soldiers and 3-4 cannons. As a result of a day-long battle in which the Polish artillery took an active part until the ammunition ran out, the Russians managed to push back the Confederate forces and successfully repel counterattacks.

Polish troops were hampered by poor training and equipment. In addition, these units were using outdated tactics – the caracole (riding past and firing into the enemy formation) instead of charging home against the enemy. A 110 Barists were killed and 120 were wounded, as well as about 1,000 Confederates deserted and fled the battlefield and were taken prisoner. The Russian forces lost 120 killed and 200 wounded.

The **Battle of Orzechowo** was fought on September 13, 1769. The Polish commanders were Antoni Pułaski, Franciszek Ksawery Pułaski and Kazimierz Pułaski who were opposed by Karol August von Rönny and Aleksandr Suvorov. The Bar forces marched to Kobryń with the intention of activating insurgent activities in the area of the Grand Duchy of Lithuania. Upon the news of Alexander Suvorov's Russian troops moving from the east and the forces of Karol August von Rönny from the southwest, the Confederates retreated south. Suvorov caught up with the Poles near Orzechowo. Though the Confederates were unaware of the smaller size of Suvorov's forces, they did not en-

Kazimierz Pułaski (1745 - 1779) by Jan Styka

gage in head on battles, but fighting retreats, mostly with infantry-based units in an area rich in forests and swamps.

Suvorov outflanked the Polish army with the help of light infantry and Cossacks, twice forcing them to leave their positions. After 7 hours of marching, interrupted by fighting, the Pulaski family finally managed to break away from the Russians. As they were crossing over the Bug, news reached the Barists about the approaching Russian troops of Rönny, and they set off at night towards Włodawa.

In Włodawa, there was a disagreement among the insurgents, which resulted in some of them moving west towards Łomazy, and the rest remained where they were. Rönny's unexpected attack from the north smashed the insurgents stationed in Włodawa. A similar fate befell the group going to Łomazy, which was turned back by part of the Suvorov drive.

Gen. Charles Francois Dumouriez (1739 - 1823) by J.J. Ryms. He was sent by France to help the Barists.

Following the battle at Orzechowo, an engagement was fought at *Łomazy* on September 15, 1769 during the retreat from Włodawa. Advancing on Łomazy was the advance guard of the Confederate army commanded by Franciszek Ksawery Pulaski. The Russian cavalry under the command of Karol August von Rönny attacked the balance of the Barist forces under the command of Kazimierz Pulaski were resting in Włodawa. Kazimierz Pułaski and Józef Miączyński organized the defense of Włodawa, but soon there was a retreat towards Łomazy.

After receiving false information from the first refugees from Włodawa that his brother Kazimierz Pułaski had been taken prisoner by Russia, Franciszek Pułaski returned. After a confused night march, the rest of the Barist forces arrived from Włodawa in the morning on September 15, 1769. The Barists were attacked by a detachment of Russian carabiniers under the command of Count Castelli, coming from Sławatycze, as well as attacked from the rear by Suvorov's cavalry and they attempted to break through from the encirclement. Kazimierz Pułaski's brother, Francis Xavier was killed during this fighting. *"In the rear, from the direction of Łomazy, Russian Carabiniers led by Castelli appeared. The Pulaskis were looking for salvation in a daring attack ... Franciszek caught up with Castellego himself, but he was fatally shot with a pistol ... in Włodawa he was buried in a mass grave by the Paulini fathers ... «.* He was probably buried on the battlefield near Łomazy, in the mass grave of the Confederates of Bar.

The **Battle of Dobra** was fought on January 23, 1770 in Greater Poland. With over 6,000 troops and 18 guns in a Barist Army under the command of the Marshal of Lublin Adam Szaniawski. He was trying to break through to Wielkopolska, using his numerical advantage and knock out the Russian army corps of 3,000 troops Col. Ivan Drewicz and Karl Gustav von Rönne. The Russians anchored against the city's outskirts, while the Barists mistakenly struck the heavily defended right wing of the tsarist troops. At the same time, the Russians attacked of the right wing of the Confederate troops, who broke and disbursed. In order to strengthening of the deteriorating Polish right wing, the Polish left flank was turned by the Russian troops, which resulted in a complete defeat of the Barist forces. Szaniawski himself was seriously wounded, many Barist commanders were taken prisoner with the loss of 1,500 troop and all the cannons. This defeat caused the many Barist troops to disband in this area, while some escaped to Cieszyn Silesia.

The **Battle of Kcynia** was fought on January 29, 1770 near Kcynia between units of the Bar Confederates under the command of Antoni Morawski , Władysław Mazowiecki , Paweł Skórzewski and Michał Władysław Lniski (many of whom would command troops during the fighting in 1792 and 1794) with approximately 2,500 men and a Russian army with 6,000 soldiers under General Piotr Czertoryżski. After a short maneuver to attack, the Russian forces overwhelmed the rebels, killing 150 of them and forcing the units to disburse, essentially ending Barist activity in Pomerania.

The **Battle of Dęborzyn** was fought on May 15, 1770 in the area of the village of Dęborzyn. Kazimierz Pułaski was leading a 1,200-strong cavalry unit during a foray towards Tarnów. The Barists took up positions on a hill overlooking a road leading through a ravine. The clash took place on Pulaski's initiative, without consulting with the Confederation leadership. The ensuing fight with the Russian army resulted in the death of 200 Barists and the retreat of their forces in the area.

Kazimierz Pulaski at Czestochowa by Jozef Chelmoski

The Defense of Jasna Góra in Częstochowa was conducted from September 10, 1770 to August 18, 1772. Kazimierz Pułaski and Michał Walewski took control of the monastery through trickery, making it a Barist base. Walewski was appointed the commander, but Pulaski held the real power. Colonel Ivan Drewitz, operating in this area with Russian troops, trying to capture the monastery. Pułaski's assistants were Major General Karol Zamoyski, Filip Radzimiński and Prior Pafnucy Brzeziński. At different points the Monastery held up to 1,450 troops and 40 cannon. At the end of 1770, Pulaski had 300 cavalry and 700 infantry in the Jasna Góra garrison. Drewicz unsuccessfully tried to conquer the monastery from December 31, 1770 to January 14, 1771. The defense of the monastery contributed to Pulaski's reputation. Jasna Góra was finally conquered by the enemies of the confederation on August 18, 1772. Control of the monastery resonated with the calls for freedom the Barists tried to pitch as Jasna Góra was the scene of defiance against the Swedes during the "Deluge" of the 17th Century.

Battle of Widawa was fought on June 23, 1771 between Barist troops led by Józef Zaremba and the royal army led by Franciszek Ksawery Branicki. This action ended with the destruction of the royal army.

King Poniatowski and the Russian Embassy suspected Hetman Ogiński of supporting the Bar Confederation. The Russian forces tried to encircle the hetman's group to surrender. Russian troops of Fabułów, Duringa and Albiczewo tried to surround Hetman's army in Telekhanach. When the Russian envoy, Major Soldenhof, demanded the surrender of the Lithuanian army, the indignant hetman arrested him, saying: "I am the Hetman of the Republic of Poland, so I should not obey foreign orders".

On the morning of September 6, the hetman surrounded Beździeż with his troops, in which the unit of Colonel Albiczew was located. At high noon, an assault was carried out with all the forces, the Russian commander was killed and his forces defeated. While the resulting the **Battle of Beździeż** was a propaganda victory for the Barists, Ogiński had only 3,000 soldiers and was not able to take control of Niasviž and Slutsk. Ogiński decided to wait for reinforcements.

The **Battle of Stołowicze** was fought on September 23, 1771 when the 822 troops of the Russian army of General Alexander Suvorov crushed a detachment of 2,500 Bar Confederates, commanded by the Grand Hetman of Lithuania, Michał Kazimierz Ogiński.

The Confederation army was deployed on the night of September 22/23 in Stołowicze with 300 of the hetman's Janissaries and 700 cavalrymen were placed in the market along with 5 cannons. On the west side of the town, two infantry units of 300 and 200 soldiers were deployed, along with 5 cannons. About 1,000 of the Bielak lancers were placed behind the town.

Suvorov prepared the infantry in two lines, with the cavalry in the rear. Four captured lancers revealed a way through the marshes to the Russians. Due to the lack of proper pickets, the alarm was raised too late, as the Russian cavalry attacked the Janissaries[2] in the town square. The Russians cut up those cut off from the lancers led by Józef Bielak (1,500 troopers). Only Bielak's cavalry managed to withdraw, as it was outside the town's buildings at the time of the attack. All Polish artillery fell into Suvorov's hands. Confederate losses amounted to 1,000 casualties. As a result of this defeat, the Barists lost its support in Lithuania, and the remaining troops of the confederation retreated towards East Prussia.

On 22 February 1771 the last major battle of the war took place at **Lanckorona**. After an unsuccessful attempt to capture the Tyniec monastery, the Russian army under General Alexander Suvorov, headed towards Lanckorona, where Confederate forces were gathering under the command of Charles Francis Dumouriez, the commander of the army of the First French Republic. Hearing about the march of Russian troops Dumouriez did mobilize a force which has been estimated by historians at around 1,300 soldiers and several cannons.

In addition to their numerical superiority, the Russian forces were more disciplined and better armed than the Barist ones. General Suvorov's forces consisted of 2 infantry regiments (Astrakhan and St. Petersburg) under the command of Colonels Drewicz and Szepelewo, as well as a cavalry unit. The Barists had a large undisciplined force that seemed eager to flee the battlefield. In addition, there were frictions between the officers in the Barists command itself. Ultimately, Dumouriez managed to gather the entire Barist army on one of the hills south of the city. General Szyc's hussars was charged to protecting against the enemy from encircling the Polish forces. The center was made up of a rifle squad, and the left wing was made up of cavalry.

The Bar Army at Lanckorona by Artur Grottger

---

[2]The Janissaries were modeled on the elite Ottoman forces. They appeared in the Commonwealth army starting during the reign of Jan Sobieski.

The tsarist army attacked from the south from the area of the village of Palcza. The Polish infantry, standing in the center of the formation, started to flee as the Russian infantry advanced. Meanwhile, the Confederate cavalry positioned on the left wing, attempted to surround Suvorov's forces and clashed with the enemy cavalry. Just like the infantry, the cavalry started to flee. The officers who tried to stop them were either trampled or slaughtered. This was the fate of Prince Kajetan Michał Sapieha and Antoni Orzeszka. The hussar regiment of General Szyc, who wanted to support the already escaping center, attacked the Russians but his forces broke down after firing one volley (which did not cause any harm to the tsarist army). The Russians, seeing the fleeing Barists, gave chase. They managed to kill about 300 Confederate fighters, mainly in the nearby grove (which was later called Groby). The Russians were close to catching up with Dumouriez but he managed to withdraw in time. Those officers who failed to do so were often exiled to Siberia).

The Barists lost about 300 soldiers in the battle, most of whom were buried in a common grave in the Groby forest while the Russian losses amounted to four to five soldiers as a result of shelling from the Lanckorona fortress.

Rejtan or The Fall of Poland, by Jan Matejko depicts the deputy Tadeusz Rejtan trying to stop the signing of the first partition of Poland by the Polish Sejm in 1773.

Operations of the Polish-Lithuanian Armies 1791-1793

The ***Battle of Opsa*** took place on 26 May 1792. The battle was fought near the tiny village of Opsa, near Brasław, Grand Duchy of Lithuania (present-day Belarus), between the Russian corps of Prince Yuri Dolgorukov and the Tatar regiment of the Grand Duchy, commanded by Michał Kirkor. The battle ended in a Russian victory, as the Lithuanians were forced to retreat and the Russians occupied Brasław.

Prince Dolgorukov's corps (9,000 soldiers) crossed the Daugava River on 22 May, with the majority of the troops and tabor crossing at Dyneburg and the rest of the troops under the command of General Johann von Rautenfeld crossed the river at Krasław. Both columns of the Russian corps then moved on Brasław.

Soon after crossing to the other bank of the Daugava, Rautenfeld sent his Don Cossacks to scout the town of Druja. Cossack intelligence indicated that a Lithuanian Tatar banner under the command of Rotmistrz Rejżewski was stationed in the town. Upon their return, the Cossacks smashed a detachment sent by Kirkor's regiment, and captured two Lithuanian Tatar uhlans. Rautenfeld immediately sent a detachment of 160 soldiers. However, when Rejżewski learned of the advancing Russians, he withdrew to Głębokie. Rautenfeld gave up the pursuit and continued to march on Brasław, which he occupied on 26 May.

There are two known accounts describing the battle of Opsa - one by Szymon Zabiełło, and the other by Józef Sułkowski.

According to Zabiełło, when Rautenfeld took Brasław, the bulk of Dolgorukov's corps marched on Opsa. The vanguard was made up of 100 Cossacks led by Captain Belogorodtsev. Belogorodtsev sent a seven-man scout detachment, who stumbled on a similar reconnaissance troop from Kirkor's Tatar regiment. This led to fighting in the vicinity of Opsa, during which Kirkor's regiment fought against a Cossack force of a few hundred men led by Colonel Kireyev. After a few hours of fighting, the Lithuanian regiment was forced to retreat. Rotmistrz Miłłaszewicz was captured, and Lieutenant Achmatowicz was severely wounded. Zabiełło

A trooper of the Polish National Cavalry vs Russian infantry, 1794. AO

believed that a few dozen Russian soldiers were killed.

Sułkowski wrote that Kirkor's regiment watched the movements of the Russian troops. Rautenfeld encircled Opsa on the night of 25 May, with the aim of neutralizing the Lithuanian Tatar force. Kirkor wanted to avoid being captured by the Russians, so he threw his regiment into a desperate attack, which allowed him to break out of the encirclement and retreat. During the

Prince Józef Poniatowski in 1792 by Józef Grassi

fighting, the Lithuanians lost 300 troops, and the Russians lost between fifty and 300 men.

The **Battle of Mir** took place in the town of Mir, which is now part of Belarus on June 11, 1792. Despite Lithuanian numerical superiority (8,000 to 5,500), they were defeated. The Russian army of Boris Mellin defeated the Lithuanian force under Józef Judycki. The confrontation could have gone the other way if the 900 troops under Stanisław Kostka Potocki and Tomasz Wawrzecki were used to augment the defence; instead Judycki called a two-hour counsel of war. This gave time for the Russian forces to regroup and they were then able to prepare a final counterattack.

On that day there was also an assault and conquest of the Mir Castle Complex. Judycki left his troops and resorted to Grodno. Disgraced Judycki was relieved of command soon afterwards, on June 17, to be replaced by Michał Zabiełło.

The **Battle of Boruszkowce** took place on 14 June 1792, between a detachment of a Polish army of Michał Wielhorski and a Russian army group under the command of Michail Kachovski.

Main Polish forces under command of Poniatowski withdrew to Połonne across the Czantoria Mountains. They were secured from the south by a division under command of Kościuszko. A Polish army train, secured by a division of Wielhorski, moved the shortest way across Boruszkowice. Wielhorski had 6,500 troops and 12 cannons under his command. The route was over marshy ground and thick with forests allowing Russian formations cover making it difficult for Polish defence. After getting information about Polish withdrawal, Mikhail Kakhovsky moved two Cossacks regiments under command of Alexey Orlov and a part of cavalry under command of Alexander Tormasov. These forces attacked and destroyed the rear of the Polish train. There were clashes between the Polish and Russian cavalry and fighting between Polish and Russian infantry and artillery. The Polish cavalry successfully defended against the first attack of Russian cavalry then withdrew. Infantry and artillery began defence of train. The collapsing of bridge on the swamp river Derevichka was a trap. Polish infantry (1,000 soldiers) and artillery successfully defended against the Russians who were able to receive reinforcements during fight. When the Polish did not get relief, they began withdrawal under enemy fire. The Polish division received heavy losses of soldiers, seven cannons, and the baggage train. The Russian were halted for several hours.

The **Battle of Zieleńce** took place on 18 June 1792, between the Polish–Lithuanian Commonwealth Army of Józef Poniatowski and an Imperial Russian Army group under the command of General Irakly Morkov, which was a part of General Mikhail Krechetnikov's Russian forces invading the Polish–Lithuanian Commonwealth from the south. The battle ended in Polish victory, as the Russian assault was repulsed, although the Poles soon withdrew from the battlefield.

Polish forces had been retreating for several weeks, avoiding a decisive engagement with the numerically superior Russian forces.

On 15 June, the joined Polish forces reached Połonne. After a meeting, the Polish commanders decided to withdraw because they did not have the possibility of defending a town that did not have fortifications. On 17 June, Polish commander Prince Józef Poniatowski received information in Szepietówka that the Lubomirski division was now camped

The Battle of Zielence - returning with captured battle standards by Wojciech Kossak

in Zasław. He ordered the Lubomirski division to join his forces near Zieleńce. Lubomirski had about 2,000 infantry and 1,000 cavalry, including units of general Józef Zajączek and Ludwik Trokin. His formation secured a hill situated on the north of the road from Połonne to Zasław which dominated the area. Infantry taking position in centre wings were secured by cavalry. In the early morning of 18 June, a Russian group under command of General Irakly Morkov was observed. This group was front watch of larger corps of General Mikhail Golenishchev-Kutuzov. The order of this group was to attack the Polish army left wing and destroy the rest of train. With a force about 10,500 -11,500 soldiers and 24 cannons (2 infantry regiments of about 6,000 soldiers, three regiments of line cavalry of 2,500 soldiers, and a Cossack brigade under command of Orlov), the Russian formations took positions in a valley below a hill. Their order of battle was the same as Polish, except that one battalion was a reserve and the second to secure the train. Meanwhile, General Zajączek contacted Poniatowski for help.

The battle began with artillery fire and cavalry clashes. About 7 a.m., Markow wanted to begin to attack but changed his orders when he saw that Polish units under Poniatowski had moved onto the battle field. Poniatowski forces included two infantry battalions, a cavalry regiment of front guard from Prince Józef Lubomirski, Brigade National Cavalry under command of Stanisław Mokronowski, a division under command of General Wielhorski, and 12 cannons. Kościuszko with his division had to stay in the rear in order to prevent an attack from Levanidov and Dunin corps. Poniatowski sent the Mokronowski brigade on right wing. He backed the artillery. The battalion of infantry regiment of Potocki was in reserve. The division of Wielhorski took position within the forest as a reserve.

After a few hours, the Polish and Russian artillery fell silent. Within 12 hours with Russian-backed artillery fire, the infantry began advancing onto the Polish centre. Under mass artillery fire and a Russian attack, panic was induced among the Polish recruits who began escaping. After some time, Józef Poniatowski reviewed the Polish position. He organized a new battalion from the Potocki regiment and with support of battalion ordnance Ostrogoski began a counterattack. Russian infantry under fire of artillery and a Polish counterattack began withdrawal incurring heavy losses. Meanwhile, another Russian infantry unit secured the village of Zieleńce and opened fire on Polish formations. Poniatowski sent a formation of cavalry, but failed. After the village was set on

Tadeusz Kościuszko by Karl G. Schweikart

fire, the Russians withdrew. Meanwhile, the Russians moved artillery fire onto Polish right wing on cavalry. The soldiers felt panic. At that moment, Cossacks began a charge. At beginning, that charge was stopped by field squadrons of Mokronowski brigade cavalry, but in formation of Regiment Buławy Koronnej panic ensued the rear squadrons of Mokronowski brigade. The panic of the Polish cavalry was stopped by Sanguszko and other officers. After reorganization, Polish cavalry with support of part Lubowidzki cavalry brigade from second line began a counter-charge. During this charge, the Polish cavalry destroyed the Russian cavalry and began to rally. Poniatowski sent an order to support the rally to Czapski commander of second line cavalry right wing. Czapski refused to obey because the order was not written. In reality the commander was sympathetic to the Targowica Confederation. During this time, a Russian regiment of grenadiers from Ekaterinoslav attacked Polish left wing. Poniatowski sent battalions from Potocki and Malczewski regiments. After decimating grenadiers under artillery and rifle fire, the Russians advance collapsed.

After collapsing the Russian advance, Poniatowski organized an attack group from division Wielhorski's units. This group contained three infantry battalions from regiments Potocki, Malczewski and Ordnance Ostrogocka, Brigade National Cavalry under command of Dzierżek, and regiment front watch under command of Józef Lubomirski. The group had to attack the Russian right wing. Morkov, who watched the preparations, concentrated most of his formation against the group. Polish cavalry successfully fought the Russian cavalry and forced them to withdrawal. But when Wielhorski met the enemy infantry, he stopped the advance because his infantry was weaker than the Russians and inexperienced. About 5 p.m. Morkov, who did not get relief from Kutuzov, withdrew.

The victorious Polish army stayed on battlefield until evening and, thereafter, withdrew to Zasław. It was a tactical victory, without much strategic implications. Polish losses were significant; soldiers lacked ammunition and food; Derdej compares it to a Pyrrhic victory. After Polish withdrawal, Morkov moved onto the battlefield and announced himself the victor. Nonetheless, modern historians classify this battle as a Polish victory.

The Russians nonetheless sustained heavier losses and were significantly delayed in their pursuit of the Polish forces. The captured Russian banner was sent to Warsaw. To commemorate this victory, Polish king Stanisław II Augustus created the order of Virtuti Militari and awarded it to a number of Polish commanders participating in that battle.

Some contemporary Polish leaders, like Kościuszko and Zajączek, felt that Poniatowski should have pursued the Russians more aggressively, but Derdej justifies his decision noting the exhaustion and low supplies of Polish forces.

The ***Battle of Dubienka*** occurred on July 18, 1792, the Polish army under the command of General Tadeusz Kościuszko defended the Bug River crossing against the Russian army under General Michail Kachovski. Although the Russians had a numerical advantage of 5:1 over the Polish defenders, their attacks were stymied by field fortifications raised by the Poles, leading to a Polish tactical victory. Subsequent Russian flanking forced the Poles to retreat to avoid being encircled. After the Polish-Lithuanian forces left their forward positions, the Russian army occupied the area.

When the Russian army invaded Poland in May 1792, they had a nearly 3:1 numerical advantage, forcing the Polish forces to retreat. General Tadeusz Kościuszko has been tasked with commanding the rear guard and delaying the Russian advance. The Bug River was the last natural obstacle before the Russian army and the Polish capital of Warsaw, about 250 km away. Kościuszko had been tasked by the Polish commander-in-chief, Prince Józef Poniatowski, with stopping a much larger Russian army attempting to cross the river near the village of Dubienka.

Kościuszko had about 5,300 forces under his command, while Russian general Michail Kachovski had about 25,000. Kachovski had also an advantage with artillery, commanding 56 cannons to Kościuszko's fewer than 10 pieces.

Kościuszko, an experienced engineer who had only recently designed the fortifications of West Point in the United States, had to secure the Bug at about 50 km of its length, on one end touching the Austrian border. He chose an advantageous position, protected by dense forests and swamps, and ordered construction of field fortifications, underwater traps, as well as burning of a nearby bridge.

Around 15:00 on 18 July the Russians reached the river, and attempted to cross it in small boats near the burned bridge, while another part of their forces crossed in the north. The initial Russian attack got bogged down in difficult terrain, and they took heavy casualties from the Polish artillery, while their own was less effective shelling the Polish fortified positions. A Russian cavalry unit made it to the Polish artillery emplacements but were pushed back, and their commanding colonel Palembach killed. After five hours of repeated assaults, the Russians retreated, leaving about 4,000 dead. The Poles took about 900 casualties, mostly from the Russian artillery fire.

After nightfall, Polish scouts reported Russians crossing to the south, through neutral Austrian territory. As the Poles were running low on supplies, Kościuszko decided that his army could

The Virtuti Militari 1792

not withstand a prolonged siege, and ordered a retreat towards Chełm to avoid being encircled.

While Kościuszko was criticized for retreating by some officers, he was rewarded by king Stanisław August Poniatowski with a Virtuti Militari order. He was also praised by his opponent, General Michail Kachovski, who in his official report noted that this was the most difficult battle of the campaign so far. One week after this battle Poland capitulated.

Operations of the Polish-Lithuanian Army 1794

Under the terms of the armistice that followed the second partition, the forces of the Polish armed forces were to be reduced to insignificant levels. It was important for the conspirators to act before the regiments - which were still in the field - were demobilized and making insurrection impossible.

The **Battle of Racławice** was one of the first battles of the Polish-Lithuanian Army in the Kościuszko Uprising against Russia. It was fought on 4 April 1794 near the village of Racławice in Lesser Poland.

General Denisov, with 2,500 troops, had planned to attack the Poles from the south, while Tormasov's force of 3,000 troops blocked Kosciuszko. Encountering Tormasov's force first, Kosciuszko occupied a nearby hill, General Antoni Madalinski on his right and General Józef Zajączek on his left. Not waiting any longer, Tormasov attacked the hill by 3:00 PM, setting up their cannon. Kosciuszko inspired his peasant brigade with shouts of "My boys, take that artillery! For God, and the Fatherland! Go forward with faith!"

Gen. Antoni Madaliński (1739 - 1805) launched the revolt ahead of schedule

The first group of serfs captured three twelve-pound cannons and the second wave captured eight more cannons. Moving to his left flank, Kosciuszko led a bayonet charge when the Russians fled, followed closely by the scythemen.

The Polish Order of Battle was as follows:

Unit	Strength
Czapski's Infantry Regiment (2nd)	400 men in 1 battalion
Wodzicki's Infantry Regiment (3rd)	400 men in 2 battalions
Ożarowski's Infantry Regiment (6th)	400 men in 2 battalions
Raczyński's Infantry Regiment (7th)	200 men in 2 companies
Antoni Madaliński's cavalry (Ist Brde)	400 men in 10 squadrons
Magnet's cavalry (IVnd Brde)	400 men in 10 squadrons
Biernacki's cavalry (IInd Brde)	160 men in 3 squadrons
Duke of Württemberg (4th Adv. Guard)	80 men in 2 squadrons

Total   2,440

In addition, Malopolska raised approximately 2,000 peasants armed with war scythes and pikes, known as Scythemen, as well as 11 cannon. The outcome of the battle was a tactical Polish victory, with Kościuszko defeating the numerically inferior enemy. However, his forces were too small to undertake a successful pursuit, and the Corps of General Denisov evaded destruction and continued to operate in Lesser Poland.

Kosciuszko marched back to Kraków and made camp in the fields of Bosutow. After the battle, Kościuszko paraded before his troops in a sukmana, a traditional attire worn in Lesser Poland, in honour of the bravery of the peasants, whose charge ensured the quick capture of the Russian artillery.

Parade in Kraków of the 12 Russian canons captured in the Battle of Racławice in 1794. MS

He also praised Wojciech Bartosz Głowacki, a peasant who was the first to capture the cannon (he is visible in Matejko's. He smothered its fuse with his hat before it fired. In return he received an award of nobility, his freedom, a tract of land and made standard-bearer.

The victory was subsequently promoted in Poland as a major success and helped in spreading the Kościuszko Uprising to other areas of Poland and instigating the Warsaw Uprising of 1794. Also, the participation of peasant volunteers was seen by many as the starting point of the Polish peasantry's political evolution from serfs to equally entitled citizens of the nation.

The ***Warsaw Uprising of 1794*** or ***Warsaw Insurrection*** was an armed insurrection by the people of Warsaw early in the Kościuszko Uprising. Supported by the Polish Army, the uprising aimed to throw off control by the Russian Empire of the Polish capital city (Warsaw). It began on 17 April 1794, soon after Tadeusz Kościuszko's victory at the Battle of Racławice.

Although the Russian forces had more soldiers and better equipment, the Polish regular forces and militia, armed with rifles and sabres from the Warsaw Arsenal, inflicted heavy losses on the surprised enemy garrison. Russian soldiers found themselves under crossfire from all sides and from buildings, and several units broke early and suffered heavy casualties in their retreat.

Kościuszko's envoy, Tomasz Maruszewski, and Ignacy Działyński and others had been laying the groundwork for the uprising

Fighting on the KrakowskiePrzedmieście in Warsaw, 1794 . JPN

Warsaw insurrection 1794 by Juliusz Kossak.

since early 1793. They succeeded in winning popular support: the majority of Polish units stationed in Warsaw joined the ranks of the uprising. A National Militia was formed by several thousand volunteers, led by Jan Kiliński, a master shoemaker.

Within hours, the fighting had spread from a single street at the western outskirts of Warsaw's Old Town to the entire city. Part of the Russian garrison was able to retreat to Powązki under the cover of Prussian cavalry, but most of it was trapped inside the city. The isolated Russian forces resisted in several areas for two more days.

Upon receiving news of Kościuszko's proclamation in Kraków (24 March) and his subsequent victory at Racławice (4 April), tension in Warsaw grew rapidly. Polish king Stanisław August Poniatowski was opposed to Kościuszko's uprising, and with the Permanent Council issued a declaration condemning it on 2 April. The King dispatched Piotr Ożarowski, who as Grand Hetman of the Crown was the second-highest military commander after the king, and the Marshal of the Permanent Council, Józef Ankwicz, to Iosif Igelström, Russian ambassador and commander of all Russian occupation forces in Poland, with a proposal to evacuate both the Russian troops and Polish troops loyal to the King to a military encampment at Nowy Dwór Mazowiecki.

Igelström rejected the plan and saw no need for the Russians to evacuate Warsaw. He sent a corps under General Aleksandr Khrushchev to intercept Kościuszko and prevent him from approaching Warsaw. He also ordered increased surveillance of suspected supporters of the uprising, and imposed censorship all mail passing through Warsaw. Igelström issued orders for the arrest of those he suspected of having any connection with the insurrection. These included some of the more prominent political leaders, among them Generals Antoni Madaliński, Kazimierz Nestor Sapieha and Ignacy Działyński, King's Chamberlain Jan Walenty Węgierski, Marshal of the Sejm Stanisław Małachowski, Ignacy and Stanisław Potocki and Hugo Kołłątaj. At the same time Russian forces started preparations to disarm the weak Polish garrison of Warsaw under General Stanisław Mokronowski by seizing the Warsaw Arsenal at Miodowa Street. These orders only made the situation worse as they were leaked to the Poles ahead of time.

The Russian forces prepared a plan to seize the most important buildings to secure the city until reinforcements arrived from Russia. General Johann Jakob Pistor suggested that the barracks of "unsafe" Polish units be surrounded, and the units disarmed, and the Warsaw Arsenal captured to prevent the revolutionaries from seizing arms. At the same time bishop Józef Kossakowski, known for his pro-Russian stance, suggested that the churches be surrounded on Holy Saturday on 19 April with troops and all suspects attending the mass be arrested.

Kościuszko already had supporters in Warsaw, including Tomasz Maruszewski, his envoy who was sent to Warsaw with a mission to prepare the uprising. Maruszewski created the Revolution Association (Związek Rewolucyjny), organizing the previously independent anti-Russian factions. The Association included among its members various high-ranking officers from the Polish forces stationed in Warsaw. Among them were Michał Chomentowski, Gen. Krystian Godfryd Deybel de Hammerau, Major Józef Górski, Capt. Stanisław Kosmowski, Fryderyk Melfort, Dionizy Poniatowski, Lt. Grzegorz Ropp and Józef Zeydlitz.

Ignacy Działyński (1754 – 1797) was commander of the 10th Infantry Regiment

Among the most influential partisans of the uprising was General Jan August Cichowski, the military commander of the Warsaw's garrison. He and General Stepan Stepanovich Apraksin devised a plan to defend the city against the revolutionaries, and convinced the Russians to leave the Arsenal, the Royal Castle and the Gunpowder Depot defended by the Polish units. A prominent burgher, master shoemaker Jan Kiliński, started gathering support from other townsfolk.

As a large part of the Polish forces consisted of irregular militia raised during the 1792 War or regular units in various stages of demobilisation, the exact number of the troops fighting on the Polish side is difficult to estimate. The Polish regular forces consisted of 3,000 infantry and 150 cavalry. The largest Polish unit was the Foot Guard of the Polish Crown Regiment with 950 men under arms. The regiment was stationed in its barracks in Żoliborz, away from the city centre, but it was also responsible for guarding the Royal Castle and some of the strategically important buildings. The 10th Regiment of Foot was supposed to be reduced to 600 men, but in April 1794 could still muster some 850 soldiers. In addition, two companies of the reduced Fusilier Regiment were stationed in the vicinity of the Arsenal and still had 248 soldiers.

The Polish forces included a variety of smaller units in various stages of demobilisation, among them the 4th Regiment of Advanced Guard cavalry, 331 men of the 5th Cavalry Regiment and 364 men of the once-powerful Horse Guard of the Polish Crown Regiment. In the eastern borough of Praga there were 680 men and 337 horses of the Royal Uhlan squadrons and the Engineering Battalion ("pontoniers"). The latter units crossed the Vistula and took part in the fighting but served as standard infantry as their horses had to be left on the other side of the river. Some historians believe that the number of townspeople serving in various irregular militia forces did not exceed 3,000. Many of them were demobilized veterans of regular Polish units who followed their units to Warsaw.

The Russian garrison of Warsaw had a nominal strength of 11,750 men, including 1,500 cavalrymen, at least 1,000 artillerymen with 39 guns and an unspecified number of Cossacks. Due to widespread corruption among Russian officers, Russian infantry battalions rarely had more than 500 men at arms instead of the nominal strength of 960. The Russian garrison had 7,948 men, 1,041 horses and 34 guns. Most of them were soldiers of the Siberian and Kiev Grenadier Regiments. In addition, Igelström could request assistance from a Prussian unit of General Friedrich von Wölcky stationed west of the city in the fields between Powązki and Marymont. The latter unit had 1,500 men and 4 guns.

After the Russian plan of surrounding the churches on Saturday was discovered by the Poles, it was decided that the uprising should start immediately. On Holy Wednesday the Polish garrison was secretly provided with volleys and artillery charges and overnight was dispatched to various parts of the city. The Russians were conscious of the preparations for the uprising and their troops were also equipped with additional ammunition. At 03:30 some 20 Polish dragoons left the Mirów barracks and headed for the Saxon Garden. They encountered a small Russian force equipped with two cannons guarding the Iron Gate, the squadron charged the Russian positions and captured the guns. Soon afterwards the remainder of the Royal Horse Guard Regiment left the barracks on foot and headed in two directions: towards the outer gates of the city at Wola and towards the Warsaw Arsenal, where the Russian forces were preparing an assault. The troops at the Arsenal was also joined by a small troop of National Cavalry under Colonel Jan Jerzy Giessler, who crossed the Vistula overnight.

Jan Kiliński (1760 - 1819)

At 05:00 the planned Russian assault on the Arsenal started but was repelled by unexpected opposition from Polish forces. After the first shots, the guards of the Arsenal started giving out arms to the civilian volunteers, who quickly joined the fights. The arsenal was secured, but the Polish plan to catch most of the Russian soldiers on the streets rather than in buildings and barracks failed. One such group armed with a cannon broke through the Warsaw's Old Town to Krasiński Square, and two others started marching along Długa Street. Their action spread the uprising to all parts of the city. Until 06:30 the regular units and the militia clashed with the Russian outposts at Nalewki, Bonifraterska, Kłopot and Leszno streets.

The initial clashes caused much confusion as not all forces involved had been notified of the plans of both sides. Among such units was the Royal Foot Guard unit, which broke through to Castle Square, where it was to await further orders. The small troop pledged to defend the monarch as soon as he appeared at the Castle's courtyard, but on hearing the sounds of a battle nearby, the unit left the king and joined the fighting at Miodowa Street; The Russian forces, pushed back after their initial failure at the gates of the Arsenal, withdrew towards Miodowa Street, where they amassed in front of Igelström's palace. There they were shelled by a small Polish force stationed in the gardens of the Krasiński Palace but destroyed the Polish unit and successfully reorganize and rally. The chaos in the Russian ranks could not be eliminated as Igelström's headquarters had been cut out from the rest of the city and he could not send a request for reinforcement to Russian units stationed outside the city centre and the Russian chain of command had been practically paralyzed. By 07:00 the confusion was partially cleared and heavy fighting at Miodowa street turned into a regular battle in the vicinity of both the Arsenal and Igelström's headquarters, as both sides struggled to secure both buildings. Three Russian assault groups, each of them battalion strength, attacked the Arsenal from three sides: from Tłomackie, along Miodowa Street and from Franciszkańska Street. All the Russian assaults were repelled with heavy losses on both sides and the Poles started a counter-attack towards the Russian positions at Miodowa, Senatorska, Leszno and Podwale Streets, but with little success.

The assault on Leszno Street was aimed at the Russian battalion occupying positions before the Carmelite Church. After several hours' heavy close-quarters fighting, the Russian forces were forced to retreat to the church itself, where fighting continued. The Russian soldiers surrendered, and only a small detachment, mostly of officers, continued the fight inside the church, where most of them perished Also the Russian battalion under Major Titov, stationed at Bonifraterska Street, had been attacked around 07:00

Fighting on Miodowa Street Street, 1794. JPN

by the Poles. After four hours' fighting, the Russians retreated towards the city's western outskirts.

At 06:00 the Polish 10th Regiment of Foot under Colonel Filip Hauman had left its barracks at Ujazdów to the south of the city centre, and started its march towards the Royal Castle. As an effect of the chaos in Russian ranks, the regiment reached Nowy Świat Street and Świętokrzyska Streets unopposed by Russian units stationed there, as the Russian commanders did not know what to do. It was stopped by a Russian force at Krakowskie Przedmieście Street, consisting of no less than 600 men and 5 pieces of artillery, and commanded by General Miłaszewicz. The Russian force was strategically dislocated on both sides of the street, in both the Kazimierz Palace (now the Warsaw University Rectorate) and before Holy Cross Church. Colonel Hauman started lengthy negotiations with the Russian commander asking him to allow the Polish forces to pass. The negotiations were broken and at 08:00 the Polish regiment assaulted the Russian positions. After a skirmish that ensued the Polish unit was partially dispersed and had to retreat. Parts of the unit under Major Stanisław Lipnicki retreated to the Dominican Church, where the fights continued. Other troop under Lieutenant Sypniewski broke through to the Branicki Palace, yet others found their way farther towards the Old Town, outflanking the Russians. Because of that, the Russian infantry under General Miłaszewicz and a small cavalry force under Prince Gagarin, though victorious, found themselves under crossfire and surrounded. In addition, a small yet loud militia force under Jan Kiliński appeared on their rear and all of the Polish units in the area assaulted the Russians from all directions, which resulted in almost complete destruction of the Russian units. General Miłaszewicz was wounded trying to retreat with the remnants of his force towards the Kazimierz Palace, while Prince Gagarin retreated with some cavalrymen towards the Saxon Garden, where they were ambushed by civilians who killed almost all of them. The 10th Regiment then reformed around noon and moved towards the Castle Square, where it took part in the fights against smaller Russian forces in the Old Town.

The victory of the 10th Regiment marked a turning point in the uprising, as it broke the morale of the Russian forces. After noon the fighting in front of Igelström's headquarters, at Miodowa Street and for the Arsenal continued as both sides drew reinforcements from all parts of the city. Russian units put up the strongest defence and although they were forced to retreat in the direction of the Franciscan church, they repelled early Polish attacks and captured the Krasiński Palace which the Poles had been using to fire on them from behind. At the same time the palace's garden remained in Polish hands and heavy fighting spread to that area as well. In other parts of the city smaller Russian forces defended themselves in isolated manors, as was the case of Szanowski's house at the Vistula in the borough of Powiśle, where a small Russian troop offered fierce resistance against the 10th Regiment until late afternoon. Nearby, a Russian force under Major Mayer, consisting of two companies, each armed with a cannon, fortified itself in the Kwieciński's Baths, where it defended itself for several hours. After repeated charges by the 10th Regiment, the Russian commander was left with no more than 80 men, with whom he retreated to the other side of the river.

In the meantime, the king and some members of the Targowica Confederation took refuge in the Warsaw Castle. Poniatowski nominated two trusted people to take command of the troops: Ignacy Wyssogota Zakrzewski became the mayor of Warsaw, and general Stanisław Mokronowski became the commander-in-chief of the Warsaw troops, but both quickly turned to support the uprising.

At the same time General Ivan Novitskiy amassed more than half the Russian forces at the western end of Jerusalem Avenue. About 4,000 men were withdrawn from there without a shot being fired. Among the units rallied there were forces that – according to the Russian plan – were to secure the entire southern part of Warsaw, including forces under Lieutenant-Colonel Kasztoliński and von Klugen, parts of Igelström's personal guard and the remnants of the force to take part in the battle against the 10th Regiment, commanded by Major Bago. Novitskiy, after several hours of wavering, organized a relief force of 3000 men and 10 cannons, and started a march towards the city centre. The column crossed Marszałkowska Street unopposed and reached Saxon Square. There it was met by a negligible unit of not more than 100 civilians armed with a single 6 pounder cannon, commanded by Captain of Artillery Jacek Drozdowski. The Polish unit opened fire from its cannon and started gradually retreating across the square towards the Brühl's Palace on its northern edge, firing all the way. At the same time the Russian commander did not issue any orders and his column simply stopped under fire. Although much inferior in numbers, training and equipment, Drozdowski's unit was not attacked by the Russian force, as Novitskiy lost control over his troops. The Russian soldiers broke ranks and entered the undefended Saxon Palace, where they seized the cellars full of alcohol. The Poles continued to shell them with artillery for almost three hours, without being attacked. When a company of the 10th Regiment returning from Powiśle appeared at Królewska Street, the Russians started a disorganized retreat towards Jerusalem Avenue, leaving Igelström to his fate.

The retreat of the Russian unit allowed the Poles to repel other assaults by Russian forces as well, including an attack by a thousand men from Warsaw's New Town towards the northern gate of the Old Town. Although the Russian force broke through to the Old Town, it had lost all its guns and more than half of its men. Also repelled were repeated assaults on the Arsenal from

Miodowa Street, under the command of General Tishchev. The Russians, approaching in three columns, did not coordinate their manoeuvres, allowing the Poles to deal with them separately. The first column under Tishchev approached the Arsenal at 15:00 from Miodowa Street. Although one of the building's turrets exploded, the Poles repelled the assault within half an hour, before the Russians had gathered reinforcements. The second Russian column approached the Arsenal through the Krasiński Gardens, but was stopped by massed fire from several cannon concealed in the bushes. The third Russian battalion, commanded by

The royal castle and Warsaw from the Wisla River in the 1770's by Bernardo Canaletto

Tishchev personally, approached the Arsenal from the west, along Leszno Street, where it was stopped by the Royal Guard. After a fierce fight, Tishchev died soon after a cannonball ripped his leg off, and the remainder of his force surrendered to the Poles.

In these circumstances the Poles began a counter-attack aimed at capturing Igelström's palace and the positions of the forces that he had around him. These included a battalion under Johann Jakob Pistor; a battalion drawn from Marywil commanded by Colonel Parfyeniev; a battalion of the famed Siberian Regiment; and some cavalry under Brigadier Baur. All but Parfyeniev's men had previously been involved in the failed assaults at the Arsenal and towards the Royal Castle, and all were battle-hardened. As the Poles took several buildings along Senatorska Street opposite the palace and fired at the Russians from the windows, the Russians could not reorganize their ranks and hid in the palace and the nearby Capuchin Church. Before 16:00, Działyński's Regiment reached Senatorska Street and began a frontal assault on the palace, but was bloodily repelled by the Russian defenders. Constant fire from the windows and roofs of nearby houses prevented them from mounting a counter-attack and both sides reached a stalemate. Because of that Igelström was left with little option but to await reinforcements from the outside, which did not happen. After dark a small unit under Major Titov broke through to Igelström, but his force was not strong enough to break the stalemate.

Unable to reach the palace, the Poles assaulted the Russian positions in front of the Capuchin Church and the adjoining monastery. The Russians withdrew to the courtyard, from where the fighting spread to the entire monastery. The Poles secured the courtyard and placed a cannon there, which allowed them to storm the monastery, but fierce hand-to-hand fighting, with heavy losses on both sides, continued until late evening. In the coming night, some smaller Russian units lost cohesion and attempted to retreat on their own. Many soldiers engaged in looting, and Krasiński's Palace was among the most prominent buildings looted by the soldiers during the Uprising.

Hanging the traitiors in Warsaw 1794. JPN

Overnight the fights in various parts of the city continued. The isolated Russian units defended themselves in houses in various parts of the city. In the early morning of 18 April, Mokronowski concentrated on the main remaining Russian stronghold in the city — the embassy at Miodowa Street. The Polish units, reinforced with the civilian volunteers, continued the repeated assaults on the building's courtyard. Although all were bloodily repelled, the Russians suffered significant losses as well, particularly by constant fire from buildings located to the other side of the street. The Russians held a small area delimited by Miodowa and Długa Streets, as well as Krasiński Square and the palace. Believing further defence of his palace was futile, Igelström left only a token force of 400 men there and withdrew to the Krasiński Palace. He planned to prepare a sortie in order to break through from the city centre, but all surrounding streets were filled with Polish troops and cannons.

Igelström requested permission to capitulate around 10:00, having been unable to command most of his troops during the uprising. After being granted a truce, he withdrew to the Prussian camp near Warsaw in Powązki, and then further away from the city, towards Karczew. The exact number of troops that retreated with Igelström is unknown and varies from source to source, but most estimates place it at between 300 and 400 men, with 8 cannons. As soon as Igelström's retreat was discovered, the assault on Russian positions was resumed. The remaining troops defending the embassy and covering Igelström's retreat eventually ran out of ammunition and their positions were overrun by 17:00 by the forces of the 10th Regiment under Kalinowski, aided by Kiliński's militia. Polish forces released political prisoners held by Russians in the basement and were able to secure most of the embassy's secret archive, covering all of Russian secret operations in Poland since 1763. Among the prominent captives taken during the final fights for the embassy was Colonel Parfyeniev. Among the captured documents were the lists of various Polish officials on the Russian payroll; many of them were later executed. The Polish forces also captured the treasury of the Russian ambassador, exceeding 95,000 golden ducats. This Polish victory marked the end of the uprising, with the last Russian units either routed or in retreat. The last small spots of Russian resistance were eliminated or surrendered on that day.

During the chaotic battle the Russian force lost 2,265 men killed and around 2,000 wounded. In addition, 1,926 Russian soldiers were taken prisoner of war, including 161 officers.

Losses among Polish regular forces amounted to between 800 and 1000 dead and wounded; civilian casualties and losses among various irregular militia units did not exceed 700.

Several factors contributed to the Russian defeat and losses. Igelström had reduced the size of the garrison, sending some of units to deal with Kościuszko's main forces, and posted his remaining regiments so incompetently that they were easily cut off from each other and overwhelmed by the Polish forces. From the onset of the insurrection, the Polish forces were aided by the civilian population and had surprise on their side; after the crowd captured the city arsenal, Russian soldiers found themselves under attack throughout the city.

Hanging of traitors at Warsaw's Old Town Market took place during this time and featured in a contemporary painting by Jan Piotr Norblin. The supporters of the Targowica Confederation, responsible for the Second Partition of Poland, became public enemies. If they could not be captured, their portraits were hanged instead.

Tadeusz Kosciuszko taking the oath to the nation in the Krakow marketplace.

General Mokronowski repeatedly begged the King, who was at the same time his cousin, to support the uprising. The king refused and power in the city was seized by the Provisional Temporary Council (Polish: Rada Zastępcza Tymczasowa) composed of Zakrzewski, Mokronowski, Józef Wybicki and Kiliński. Mokronowski was soon removed from the council for his opposition to Kościuszko. On 27 May the council was dissolved, and power passed to Kościuszko's Supreme National Council (Polish: Rada Najwyższa Narodowa). On 9 May four prominent supporters of the Targowica Confederation, including Józef Ankwicz, Józef Kossakowski, hetman Piotr Ożarowski and hetman Józef Zabiełło, were sentenced to death by the Insurrectionary Court and were hanged in Warsaw. A few weeks later, on 28 June, an angry mob stormed the prisons and hanged other supporters of Targowica, including bishop Ignacy Jakub Massalski, prince Antoni Stanisław Czetwertyński-Światopełk, ambassador Karol Boscamp-Lasopolski and others. Felix Potocki was not found; his portrait was hoisted on the gallows instead. Kosciuszko quickly put an end to the lynch mob declaring, "What happened in Warsaw yesterday filled my heart with bitterness and sorrow ...Those who do not obey the laws are not worthy of liberty."

The National Militia of Warsaw grew to over 20,000 men at arms and constituted a large part of the Polish Army fighting against Russia. This included 1,200 horsemen organized by Peter Jazwinski and 6,000 under Kiliński.

In the 19th century the Uprising of 1794 was presented in Imperial Russian historiography, as a "massacre" of unarmed Russian soldiers by Warsaw's mob. The defeat in this battle is sometimes seen as one of the reasons for the massacre of Praga, in which the Russian forces killed between 10,000 and 20,000 civilians of Warsaw upon their reconquest of the city later that year.

Michał Wielhorski (1755 - 1805) by Augustin Ritt

The ***Vilnius Uprising of 1794*** began on April 22, 1794, during which Lithuanian forces led by Jakub Jasiński fought Russian forces occupying the city during the Kościuszko Uprising. The Russians were expelled from Vilnius, and thanks to Jasiński's skill, no casualties were sustained during the bloodless uprising. Vilnius townspeople also actively participated in the city's defense from the Russians, some even by throwing stones at them.

A Russian garrison of some 2,000 was stationed in the spring of 1794 in the city of Vilnius, while Commonwealth forces had only 400 soldiers. In the night of April 11 / 12, upon order of Russian General Nikolai Arseniev, several rebels were arrested. On April 21, Lithuanian Hetman Szymon Kossakowski came to Vilnius, urging the Russians to capture yet more rebels, and attack rebel forces concentrated around the city. Under the circumstances, Jakub Jasinski decided to initiate the insurrection. It began in the night of April 22 / 23, and after a short fight, the city was under rebel control.

On April 24 the "Act of Rebellion of the Lithuanian Nation" was announced. The rebels declared their unity with the Kosciuszko Uprising, which had begun in Lesser Poland. On the same day, April 24, the so-called High Temporary Council was created, headed by the Mayor of Vilnius, Antoni Tyzenhauz, and Voivode of Navahrudak, Jozef Niesiolowski. It had 31 members, and formed separate offices to manage the military forces, the administration and the treasury. Jakub Jasinski was named commandant of rebel forces in the Grand Duchy of Lithuania. On April 25, Great Hetman of the Grand Duchy of Lithuania Szymon Marcin Kossakowski was hanged as a traitor of the Commonwealth.

On June 4 Tadeusz Kosciuszko dissolved the Council, as he regarded it too radical, and replaced it with Central Office of the Grand Duchy of Lithuania. Also, Kosciuszko dismissed Colonel Jasinski, naming General Michal Wielhorski commandant of the rebel army in Lithuania. Even the Lithuanian nobles of Vilnius helped in digging of the defensive lines near the city in anticipation of the Russians return. On July 19, the Russians attacked Vilnius The city was defended by 500 soldiers and 1,500 armed members of the municipal militia. Russian army, commanded by General Gotthard Johann von Knorring, had some 8,000 soldiers, with several cannons. After two days of heavy fighting, Vilnius remained in the hands of the rebels.

On August 11, General von Knorring, whose forces had grown to 12,000 soldiers, initiated another assault on Vilnius. The city, whose defense was commanded by General Antoni Chlewiński, capitulated after one day.

The 1794 ***Greater Poland Uprising*** was a military insurrection by Poles in Greater Poland against Kingdom of Prussia which had taken possession of this territory after the 1793 Second

Partition of the Polish–Lithuanian Commonwealth.

The outbreak of Kościuszko Uprising in central Poland in March 1794 served as the spark for the formation of Polish military units in the Prussian partition, as Poles in Wielkopolska hoped to liberate their region. Initially, Tadeusz Kościuszko, who had initiated the fight against Russians in central Poland did not want to support the Greater Poland Uprising in the hope of avoiding a two front war (at the time, Kingdom of Prussia was nominally in an alliance with Poland against Russia). As a result, the planned insurrection in Wielkopolska almost ended before it could start. However, the situation changed in June 1794 when the Prussians declared their support for Tsarist Russia and offered them military support in suppressing Kościuszko (after his victory at the Battle of Racławice). As a result, the Supreme National Council issued a proclamation To the Citizens of Greater Poland calling them to arms.

Józef Niemojewski (1769 - 1839)

The initial center of the uprising was the Kujawy region. The command was given to Józef Niemojewski, although many of the units in the field operated independently. Initial clashes took place on 20 August. On 22 August the insurrectionists took Gniezno. Soon after, general Paweł Skórzewski took Konin and other towns in the area. As a result, the King of Prussia, Frederick William II was forced to withdraw some of his forces from central Poland which were besieging Warsaw.

A Polish corps under Jan Henryk Dąbrowski captured Bydgoszcz on 2 October and entered Pomerania almost unopposed. Dąbrowski planned to winter in Bydgoszcz and then move through Toruń, but because of Kościuszko's defeat at the Battle of Maciejowice he decided instead to evacuate Wielkopolska and make his way into central Poland. Although thanks to the mobility of his forces he evaded being encircled by a much less mobile Prussian army, the Prussians recaptured most of the gains made by the insurrectionists in the previous few months.

Dąbrowski unsuccessfully tried to convince Kościuszko's successor, Tomasz Wawrzecki to move the insurrection from central Poland to the Prussian partition. On 17 November 1794, the last Polish units in central Poland capitulated to the Russians at Radoszyce. In Wielkopolska sporadic guerrilla fighting continued until mid-December. The uprising almost got a second life when a hero of the fighting in Warsaw and one of Kościuszko's colonels, the shoemaker Jan Kiliński (who had been born in Trzemeszno), arrived in Wielkopolska to try to reorganize the Polish forces. However, he was soon captured by the Prussians and handed over to the Russians.

The **Battle of Szczekociny** was fought on 6 June 1794 near the town of Szczekociny, Lesser Poland, between Poland and the combined forces of the Russian Empire and Kingdom of Prussia. Polish forces were led by Tadeusz Kościuszko, and the Russians and Prussians by Alexander Tormasov, future eminent general of the Napoleonic Wars. Tormasov was aided by Prussian General

Francis Favrat, who emphasized the use of artillery, which put Russian-Prussian forces in the advantage.

Following the Russian defeat at the Battle of Raclawice, the Prussians entered Poland to help confront the Polish revolt. Prussia and Russia were threatened by the sanctuary Poland offered serfs and Prussia was additionally threatened by their burghers lured to Poland's promise of democracy and free-market economy.

On the morning of 6 June, General Wodzicki noted, "It is impossible that Denisov could have amassed such an army. My eyes must be wrong, but I can see Prussians." Kosciuszko had received assurances the Prussians would remain neutral. Russian forces were placed on the left wing, while Prussian army was located on the right wing.

Battle of Szczekociny

The combined Russo-Prussian forces of 26,500 were victorious, defeating Kosciuszko's army of 15,000 with cannon fire. Polish peasant hero, Wojciech Bartosz Głowacki, died of the wounds he sustained during this battle. Other Polish military commanders who took part in the battle were General Adam Poninski, General Antoni Madalinski, General Jan Grochowski and Duke Eustachy Sanguszko. Apart from Glowacki, two Polish generals died in the battle: Jozef Wodzicki and Jan Grochowski.

The wounded Kosciuszko was found on the battlefield by General Sanguszko and stated, "I want to die here", as he was ridden to safety. The rebels retreated to Warsaw while the combined Russian and Prussian force captured Krakow on 15 June. Austria then invaded Poland from the south. The Polish revolt was reduced to defending Warsaw.

The **Battle of Chełm** was fought on 8 June 1794 between Poland and the combined forces of the Russian Empire and Prussia. The Polish were led by Józef Zajączek, the Russo-Prussian forces by Petrowicz Zagriażski and Wilhelm Derfelden. The Russo-Prussian forces consisted of 16,500 soldiers, and 24 cannons, while the Polish general only had about 6,000 soldiers, 14 cannons, and 2,000 peasant soldiers armed with war scythes.

Zajączek occupied the forested hills 1.5 km away from the city. In the early noon the Russian troops started the attack. After several hours of fighting Zajączek could only try to save as much of his army as possible through a withdrawal. In the battle, the Polish forces lost between 1,400 and 1,600 men. The Russian forces lost only about 200 men and were victorious.

The ***Battle of Rajgród*** took place on 10 July 1794 between Polish–Lithuanian army and the Kingdom of Prussia. Using only the small arms and without the heavy artillery the Commonwealth forces were able to temporarily push out the Prussian army from the city.

The ***Siege of Warsaw of 1794*** was a joint Russian and Prussian siege of the capital of the Polish–Lithuanian Commonwealth, during the Kościuszko Uprising in the summer of 1794. It ended with the Polish victory when, after a two-month siege, the Prussian and Russian army ended the siege and withdrew from Warsaw.

Józef Zajączek (1752 - 1826)

Warsaw, the capital of the Polish–Lithuanian Commonwealth, was one of the key strategic areas for all sides in the Kościuszko Uprising. Secured by the Poles during the Warsaw Uprising in April, it was threatened by the forces of the Imperial Russia and Kingdom of Prussia. Tadeusz Kościuszko, gathered forces to defend Warsaw, and around 7 to 11 July fought a delaying battle at Raszyn.

Kościuszko was able to gain some time to finish preparation for the upcoming siege, dividing his forces into the field army (23,000), garrison (3,000) and city militia (18,000). Another estimate gave him 35,000 men and 200 guns. The field army had a line of field fortifications and trenches prepared outside the main city walls and fortifications.

The besieging forces were commanded by King Frederick William II of Prussia, whose army numbered about 25,000 and 179 guns, with a Russian army of about 65,000 and 74 guns under Johann Hermann von Fersen. Another estimate gives the Prussian size at 30,000 and the Russian, at 13,000.

The attackers decided to delay their assault, waiting for heavy artillery. They launched their first attack on July 27 in the direction of Wola but were pushed back by a division under Prince Józef Poniatowski. To relieve the pressure of the siege, Kościuszko ordered the Uprising in Greater Poland, which succeeded in disrupting the Prussian forces. Kościuszko became more radical in his political influence, endorsing the Polish Jacobins to gather more popular support. The second assault by the besieging Prussian and Russian armies on 26 to 28 August was also defeated, and with the spreading of unrest in Greater Poland, Frederick William II ordered his forces to end the siege and withdraw. The Prussians would retreat to the Bzura river, while the Russians, under von Fersen, would camp near the southern Pilica river region.

The Polish victory at Warsaw is seen as one of the major accomplishments of Kościuszko, and one of the two greatest Polish victories in the Uprising, second to the success of the Greater Poland Uprising itself, which was inspired by the siege.

Despite this victory, the Uprising would soon end with Kościuszko's defeat at the battle of Maciejowice in October followed by the bloody taking of Warsaw in November.

Siege of Warsaw showing the scythemen in the trenches, 1794 by Aleksander Orlawski

The **Battle of Brest** or the **Battle of Terespol** was a battle between Russian imperial forces and Polish rebels south-west of Brest (near the village of Terespol), present-day Belarus, on 19 September 1794.

Before 19 September, Polish rebels fortified themselves in the marshes near the town of Brest. At night (at 2 AM, according to one source), Alexander Suvorov moved his troops near the Polish positions and attacked at dawn. The fighting lasted for six hours, often involving hand-to-hand combat, but the Russians finally managed to gain the upper hand, destroying the Polish force. Five hundred of Sierakowski's men were taken prisoner, and the fields all around Brest were covered with corpses. The Polish lost all of their 28 artillery pieces and two banners. According to Russian sources, Sierakowsky himself fled to Siedlce with a detachment of his cavalry corps. A Russian military report stated that losses on their side stood at 95 killed and 228 injured, however in reality it is estimated that around 1,000 Russians were killed.

The Russian victory at Brest took a major hit on Polish morale. Tadeusz Kościuszko himself was distraught by the loss. In August, he announced at a meeting that by September, the Ottoman Empire would declare war on Russia and that "Suvorov, occupied by [them], could not be in Poland." Subsequently, there were rumors that a relatively low-ranking Cossack general named Suvorov, as opposed to the well-known one, was going to lead the Russian fight in Poland. After the Battle of Brest, however, it became clear which Suvorov was on the front lines.

Kościuszko rushed to Siedlce to rally his troops and prevent the spread of panic. He explained the defeat at Brest as not the fault of the Polish commanders, but rather that the Russians simply had a numerical superiority. He also presented several of his commanders with new awards, with golden rings inscribed with the slogan, "The fatherland to its defender". Kościuszko found it necessary to remind his subordinates of their historical legacy:

> *Some tens of your ancestors could have conquered the entire Muscovite state, brought their czars in shackles, appointed the Muscovites a lord - but you, descendants of those very Polacks [sic], may doubt the successes of a fight for the fatherland, freedom, and your houses, for blood-relatives and for friends, and consider undefeatable those predatory gangs, who take the upper hand on you only because of your cowardice.*

The **Battle of Maciejowice** was fought on 10 October 1794, between Poland and the Russian Empire. The Poles were led by Tadeusz Kościuszko. Kościuszko with 6,200 men, who planned to prevent the linking of three larger Russian corps, commanded by generals Fyodor Denisov, Iwan Fersen and Alexander Suvorov. He also had requested the support of Adam Poniński (who had 4,000 soldiers), but Poniński failed to arrive on the battlefield in time.

Kosciuszko had spent the night in an abandoned manor house of the Zamoyskis with his army in the field in front flanked by woods, and a river behind the house. Denisov and then Fersen attacked the next morning, and the Poles

The Battle of Maciejowice by Jan Plersz, showing Kosciuszko being wounded by Russian cavalry.

burned the village on their left flank to prevent it being used as cover. Initially, the Russian advance was slowed by the mud, but after three hours the Poles ran out of ammunition for their cannons. The Russian infantry then made a bayonet charge and slaughtered the Poles for the next three hours.

Kosciuszko being carried from the field at Maciejowice. JPN

After three horses were shot from under him, Kosciuszko finally tried leaving the battlefield, but his horse tripped. A Cossack stabbed him with a pike from behind, followed by a second Cossack who stabbed him in the left hip. Attempting to take his own life, Kosciuszko found his pistol empty, and then passed out in the mud, but was not identified as the Polish commanding general. He was stripped by two unknown horsemen, but then saved and carried away from the battlefield by Denisov's Cossacks and later taken prisoner.

Kosciuszko was taken to St. Petersburg by General Alexei Khrushchev and two thousand Russian soldiers. The news of the fall of Warsaw reached him on 17 November.

The **Battle of Praga** or the **Second Battle of Warsaw** of 1794 was a Russian assault on Praga, the easternmost suburb of Warsaw, during the Kościuszko Uprising in 1794. It was followed by a massacre (known as the Massacre of Praga[a]) of the civilian population of Praga.

After the Battle of Maciejowice General Tadeusz Kościuszko was captured by the Russians. The internal struggle for power in Warsaw and the demoralization of the city's population prevented General Józef Zajączek from finishing the fortifications surrounding the city both from the east and from the west. At the same time, the Russians were making their way towards the city.

55

The fight at Praga, 1794 by Aleksander Orlowski

The Russian forces consisted of two battle-hardened corps under Generals Aleksandr Suvorov and Ivan Fersen. Suvorov took part in the recent Russo-Turkish war, then in the heavy fighting in Polesie and finally in the Battle of Maciejowice. Fersen fought for several months in Poland but was also joined by fresh reinforcements sent from Russia. Each of them had approximately 11,000 men.

The Polish-Lithuanian forces consisted of a variety of troops. Apart from the rallied remnants of the Kościuszko's army defeated in the Battle of Maciejowice, it also included a large number of untrained militia from Warsaw, Praga and Vilnius, a 500-man Jewish regiment of Berek Joselewicz as well as a number of scythemen and civilians. The forces were organized in three separate lines, each covering a different part of Praga. The central area was commanded directly by General Józef Zajączek, the northern area was commanded by Jakub Jasiński and the southern by Władysław Jabłonowski. Altogether, Warsaw was defended by had 30,000 men and 104 cannons. Suvorov came to the walls of Praga with 16,000 troops and 86 cannons.

The Russian forces reached the outskirts of Warsaw on 3 November 1794. Immediately upon arrival, they started an artillery barrage of the Polish-Lithuanian defenses. This made Józef Zajączek think that the opposing forces were preparing for a long siege. However, Suvorov's plan assumed a fast and concentrated assault on the defenses rather than a bloody and lengthy siege.

At 3 o'clock in the morning of November 4, the Russian troops silently reached the positions just outside the outer rim of the field fortifications and two hours later started an all-out assault. The defenders were completely surprised and soon the defence lines were broken into several isolated pockets of resistance, bombarded by the Russians with canister shots with a devastating effect. General Zajączek was slightly wounded and retreated from his post, leaving the remainder of his forces without command. This made the Poles and Lithuanians retreat towards the centre of Praga and then towards Vistula.

The heavy fighting lasted for four hours and resulted in a complete defeat of the Polish-Lithuanian forces. Joselewicz survived, being severely wounded, but almost all of his command was annihilated; Jasiński was killed fighting bravely on the front line. Only a small part managed to evade encirclement and retreated to the other side of the river across a bridge; hundreds of soldiers and civilians fell from a bridge and drowned in the process.

After the battle ended, the Russian troops, against the orders given by Suvorov before the battle, started to loot and burn the entire borough of Warsaw in revenge for the slaughter of the Russian Garrison in Warsaw during the Warsaw Uprising in April 1794, when about 2,000 Russian soldiers died, even though they died fighting as occupiers in a captive city. This propaganda was played up among the Russian forces who used that as an excuse to run rampant.

Almost all of the area was pillaged and inhabitants of the Praga district were tortured, raped and murdered. The exact death toll of that day remains unknown, but it is estimated that up to 20,000 people were killed. Suvorov himself wrote: "The whole of Praga was strewn with dead bodies, blood was flowing in streams." It was thought that unruly Cossack troops were partly to blame for the uncontrolled destruction. Some Russian historians have claimed that Suvorov tried to stop the massacre by ordering the destruction of the bridge to Warsaw over the Vistula river with the purpose of preventing the spread of violence to Warsaw..

After the battle the commanders of Warsaw and large part of its inhabitants became demoralized. To spare Warsaw the fate of its eastern suburb, General Tomasz Wawrzecki decided to withdraw his remaining forces southwards and on November 5. He supposedly was the last to leave, waving off the Russians as he left. Warsaw was captured by the Russians with little or no opposition. After the battle General Aleksandr Suvorov sent a report to Catherine the Great consisting of only four words: Hooray! Warsaw is ours! The Empress of Russia replied equally briefly: Bravo Field Marshal, Catherine, promoting him to Field Marshal for this victory. All the soldiers that took part in the sack received a commemorative medal.

The butchery by the Russian troops in Praga damaged their reputation in some eyes in Europe. Russian historians have sometimes cited the attack on the Russian troops in Warsaw as justification for the actions in Praga. The fact is the troops were not attacked on their way to church or without arms, but as an occupying army in a hostile capital. While sacking cities was common in earlier centuries it was not considered, "cvilized" in 18th century Europe.

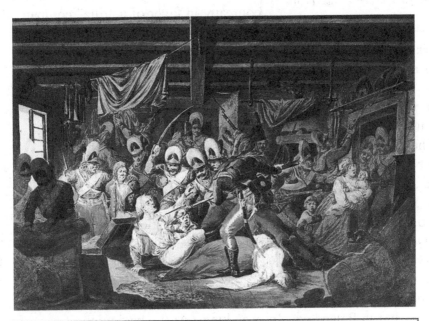

Massacre of Praga by Aleksander Orlowski, 1810. This image represents the ravages the Russian troops were allowed to perpetrate against hte civilians.

IV. Field Tactics

Queen Jadwiga Infantry in the 1770's by Raspe

Following the defeats following the Great Northern War, and despite the Saxon Kings being allied with eventual victor, Peter the Great, the Polish-Lithuanian nation had its army reduced by treaty and was essentially made a Russian protectorate. There were several attempts to reform and enlarge the army through the first half of the 18th century.

Because of the distances involved in the size of the Commonwealth, the army was anchored by units of infantry with the cavalry acting as a rapid response force. The infantry was modeled on Saxon and subsequently Prussian doctrine, which up to the 1790 reforms consisted of musketeer companies and a grenadier company. Typically, in German armies when multiple regiments were serving in the field the Grenadier Companies were joined together to form a provisional battalion to deliver a decisive stroke, but this did not seem to occur in Polish battles. Following the reforms of the Long Sejm, Commonwealth infantry dropped the Grenadier company in favor of a "rifle" company that would scout and skirmish in front of the main battle line. By the 1780's manual of arms based on the Prussian regulation was developed for the infantry.

In addition to traditional line infantry several independent companies existed in the Commonwealth forces unique to the country. There was a regiment of "fusiliers" traditional a lighter armed unit, but not unlike musketeers, that were associated with the artillery. There were also companies of Janissaries and Hajduks that served as bodyguards for the Hetman's and the King. Hajduk infantry served as the main force for Polish infantry in the 15th and 16th centuries. Janissary companies were added in the 17th century in imitation of the Ottoman troops that Polish armies came into contact with and were dressed like them much like zouave unit raised during the civil war in imitation of the French and Algerian units to give then a certain elan.

Cavalry was always the "noble" arm of troops as with many other armies, but in Poland cavalry was king. At the beginning of the century there were still banners (companies) of armored hussars and less armored pancerni, light cavalry and dragoons. Hussars and pancerni lost much of their armor as the century progressed so that by the War of Polish succession they might have been limited to helmets and breast plates. Hussar banners consisted of two types of

Towarzysz in a cape from 1790

troops – *Towarzysz* (Comrades) and *Pocztowy* (Retainer) which dates back to the 16th century. The *Towarzysz* used the lance as the primary weapon in battle followed up with a sabre and latter, pistols. By this period the Pocztowy were often but not always armed with the lance but did have a sabre and a carbine. Their main job was to charge home to overrun the enemy. By the end of the first partition, the banners were organized into "National Cavalry Brigades" of twenty-four banners so that they were large impactful formation

Light cavalry consisted of Cossack cavalry, lightly armed cavalry with lances at the beginning of the period and by the 1750's some units were organized into "Advanced Guard" (*Przedniej Straży*) which were organized as regiments, but along the lines of the National Cavalry Brigades. They operated, as scouts and skirmishers, but could also take their place in the battle line.

Dragoons were a traditional formation of Commonwealth forces dating back to the 17th century. Dragoons were a "medium" cavalry formation that could scout, ride into a place of battle and dismount to fight like infantry or charge with a sword and

Pocztowy in 1790

musket like line cavalry. Dragoons were formed as regiments in 1717, but by the late 1770's they were starting to be converted to infantry regiments and by 1789 some were converted to Advanced Guard regiments.

The artillery was divided into field and siege artillery. New cannon was not cast in the Commonwealth following the end of the Great Northern War until the 1780's when the King championed the renewal of industrial output in the nation. In the field, regiments might have a small caliber 2-3 lb cannons attached to them. Batteries were formed from four to eight pieces. For field pieces the sizes were: 12 lbs, 8 lbs., 6 lbs and 4 lbs. – which was the weight of the shot and fired in a line, which 6in and 8 in. howitzers fired a ball in an arc. Field pieces were placed in the battle line with several pieces held in reserve. Many of the barrels were made of bronze.

In addition to field pieces, heavier guns were used for sieges and against encampments. Theses could range from 12 lb. to 48 lbs. There were also small mortars that could be used in the filed or in sieges. The cannons used were a mixture of Polish made, captured pieces from French, Prussian and Russian manufacture. For the most part armies operating in the field would have under-strength artillery. At the time of the 1792 campaign there were more than 200 guns available, but they could not all be placed in the field at one time. Equipment was painted red in the Saxon according to Saxon tradition, but by the 1780's this was changed to green, and the equipment was repainted gradually as needed through repair and replacement.

The cannons were moved by an artillery train of caissons. Originally these might be private contractors attached to the army. Eventually they were an official part of the army.

During battle cannon were used as both anti-personel and counter-battery fire. Cannons were used against infantry annd cavalry in the forms of shells and canister. Shells could be solid shot or explosive. These would be fired at or above enemy units inflicting casualties on tigth formations. Canister was a bad or can of small projectives, fired at short range like a big shotgun. Artillery was also used in counter-battery fire - to take out the enemy artillery and control more of the firepower on the battle field. Counter-battery fire was usually only possible with higher caliber guns.

In the field during the first part of the century, infantry was positioned in the center, with the grenadiers on the right flank. Artillery might be positioned on the flanks or in front of the infantry. Cavalry secured the flanks and were kept in reserve. Some light cavalry might act as skirmishers ahead of the main battle force.

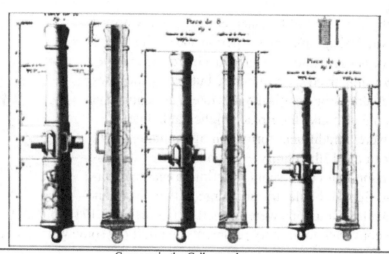

Cannons in the Gribeauval system

An officer of the Crown National Cavalry (left), an ensign standard bearer of the Lithuanian Advance Guard (center) and a Towarzysz of the Crown National Cavalary (right) - 1785.

The first infantry manual for the Commonwealth forces, published in 1790 and based on the Prussian manual. It stressed the idea of the nation.

With the reforms of the 1790s regiments would have a light infantry company that would skirmish ahead of the main battle line and could take their place in the main battle line. This is in line with changes in battle strategies on the continent and as a result of experiences in the American Revolution. These tactics would eventually be perfected by the French Armies of the Revolutionary wars, whereas Prussian doctrine rejected the mass use of light troops based on Frederick the Great's ideas. The Advance Guard regiments would harass the enemy flanks while the National Cavalry units would be used to charge a shaken or beaten enemy.

Soldiers from the Kościuszko Uprising by Stachowicz. The first and fourth figures are officers in Biernacki's regiment, the second figure is Gen. Kniaziewicz, the third is a staff officer and the figure to the right is a soldier in Wodzicki's regiment.

V. Equipment

The chaos of the early part of the 18th century took its toll on industry in Poland-Lithuania so that when Stanislaus Augustus ascended the throne there were few foundries or means to produce armament. Stanislaus tried to restart production so that Polish small arms and connon were being produced, but not in sufficient numbers to help the Commonwealth by 1792.

In the early part of the period French, Prussian, Austrian and probably some Russian muskets were in use. This created problems with supply as the caliber of the bullets ranged between .69 and .78.

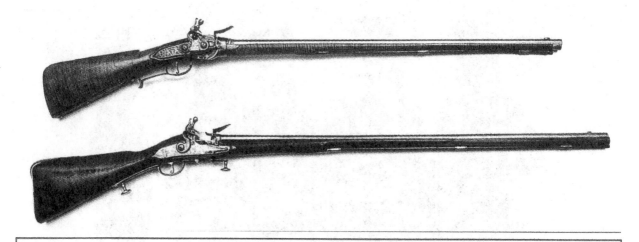

Examples of muskets in use from the 1720's.

The Charleville and Potzdam muskets were two of the most popular muskets from 1717 to the 1790's. Light infantry often had Jäger type rifles as rifled muskets were not available in large number.

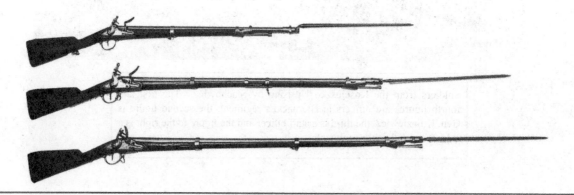

Charleville cavalry carbine, dragoon rifle and the infantry musket 1717 - 1812

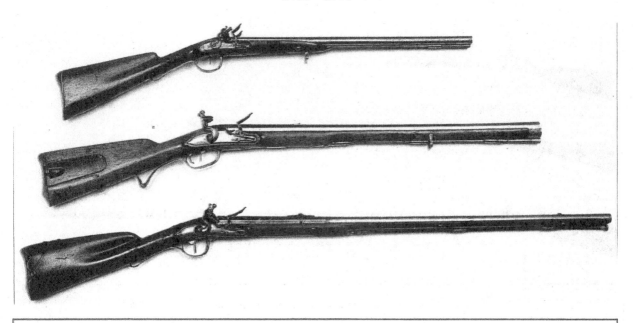

(Above) Polish made arms after the reforms of Stanislaus Poniatowski - a shotgun, sharpshooters rifle and a musket. (Below) the musketlock of a Polish made musket.

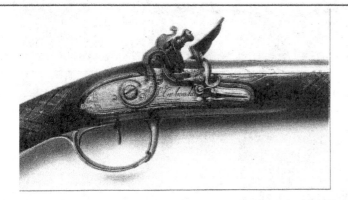

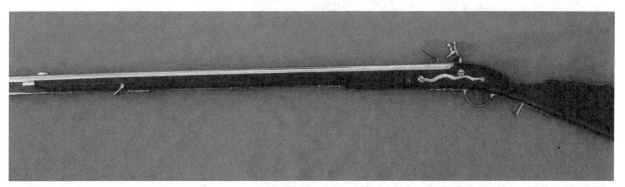

Potzdam Musket 1717 - 1807

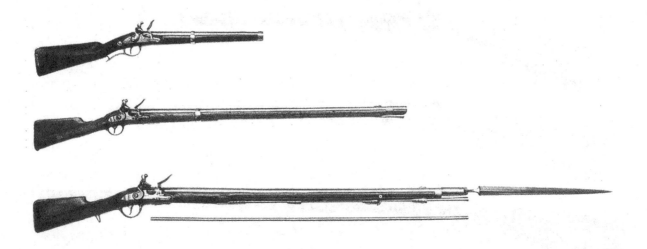

Potzdam arsenal - cavalry carbine, dragoon musket and infantry musket from the 1790's.

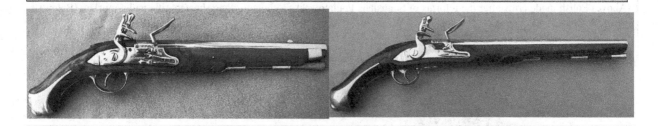

(Left) French military pistol, 1733, (right) Prussian Poztam cavalry pistol 1731. Both .62 caliber

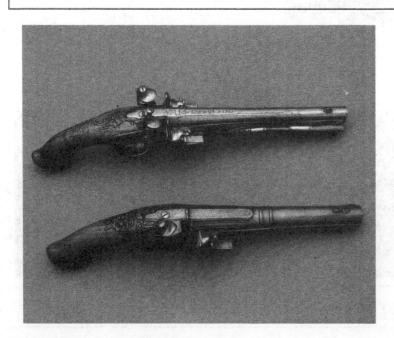

(Left) Military pistols made in Poland based on the French and Prussian designs

Swords were long associated with the nobilty and there were several model swords in use. Some officers in the infantry sued the small sword that was in use throughout the continentat this point. The cavalry used sabres in two models. The traditional cavalry sabre was the karabella which was based on asian designed and was used by the Hussars of the 17th century and the cavalry sabre with a closed guard.

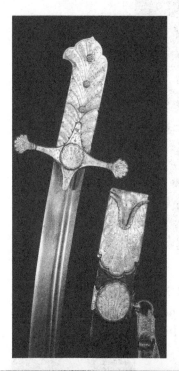
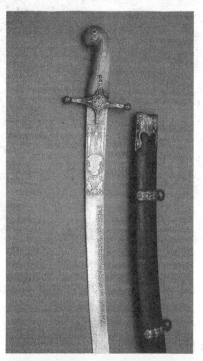

(Top left) Karabella sabre with mother of pearl hand grip, inlaid with gold from the early 18th century. (Top middle) Polish karabella made in Lwiw with a gold image of the Madonna and greek inscription, 17th/18th century. Sabre dated 1713 whch belonged to the Voivode of Krakow, Duke Janus Wisnoiwecki (1678 - 1741). (Above) Cavalry sabre of the later half of the 18th century.

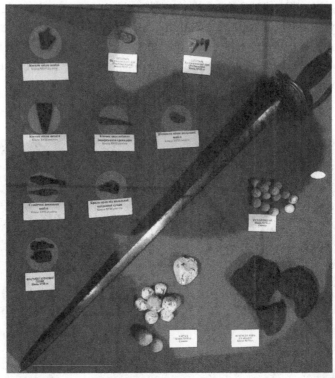

(Above) Items from the Zielence Battlefield including an infantry short sword. Courtesy of Oleg Pogorelec, Director of Panstawowy rezerwat historyczno - KuHuralny Miedzyboz.

(Left/Right) Spontoons were originally a weapon carried by NCO's and officers that could be used in combat. By the 18th century Spontoons were more cerimonial weapons, but used to allign troops in combat. The Spontoon on the left was carried by the guards in the 1730's. The one on the right was carried by an infantry unit in the 1760's.

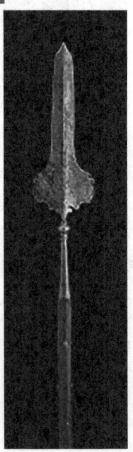

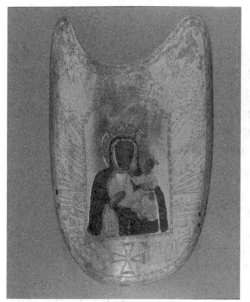 

As armor began to disappear some troops, particularly officers retained a small metal piece which was mounted around the front of the throat called a "gorget" (Which means throat), and often covered the sturnum. These were usually hightly decorative and were held in place by ribbons. The gorget on the left is from a Bar confederate. The right gorget is from the early 18th century that has the Polish eagle with the quarterings of the Commonwealth

Medals and decorations began to be introduced during this period for meritorious service - being much cheaper than land grants. The Order of the White Eagle (Left) was instituted by August II in 1705 and initially awarded to the king's closest diplomatic and political supportes. The Virtuti Militari was created by Stanislaus Augustus in 1792 to honor soldiers in the War in Defense of the Constitution. It was initially a medal - gold for officers, silver for NCO's and enlisted men. It was later isssused as a cross and is the oldest military award in the world still in use.

VI. Officers and Ranks

Throughout this period officers came primarily from the nobility, and officers of higher rank came exclusively from the nobility, so their dress reflected the wealth they might have had. Emblems of rank were traditionally a sash wore at the waist or over the shoulder. A mace or small axe was often carried as a Badge of office and the Hetman were give a Bulawa (Buława) which can be viewed as a Marshal's baton in the 19th century. Other items indicating rank were gorgets – small metal plates worn around the neck reminiscent of armor, and in some cases breastplates. Infantry officers would have a sword to direct troops, but some would also have halberds or spontoons.

Officers also often had lace around their hands in gold or silver, as well as the lapels and cuffs. Plumes were also a favorite way of displaying finery – wealth. By the 1790's Polish-Lithuanian general officers had adopted the Saxon zig-zag lace for the collar and turnbacks. By the mid-century officers began to adopt epaulettes to indicate their ranks.

Non-Commissioned officers could have their rank indicated by a worsted epaulette or a sash. In the early and mid-part of the century they might have a spontoon or halberd to keep the men in a firing line. But this would be abandoned in favor of a musket or musketoon and sword.

Figures based on the Mock painting, the King's Chamberlain (left), the Adjutant-General (center) and a Field Adjutant (right) in 1732.

(Left) Crown Hetman Albert Rzewuski in a crimson zupan and pale zupan; scarlet shoes with a blue sash - 1760. (center left) Michael Suffszynski in 1759. Metal breastplate with gilding. Yellow coat and trousers. Silver sashes with crimson threads. Black hat with silver braid and white bow. (center rigth) General in western dress from the 1740's. (Right) General in cloak - crimson.

Major Generals based on Raspe's works for the years 1777 - 1785. On the left is a major general In the center is a Hetman and on the right in a general of the artillery. All three are in western dress.

Adjutant General based on images from Raspe and Canaletto. The Adjutant General (left) in western dress, (center) in Polish dress from 1779 and (right) from 1768.

A tricorne hat of a general in the Guard Cavarly at the time of Stanislaw Augustus Poniatowski - about 1780. MWPW

The Bulawa of Field Crown Hetman Marcin Kalinowski. MWPW

Officers of the Crown Guard Cavalry in parade dress. White uniforms with a redand silver tabular, red turnbacks and blue sash. (Left) Stanislaus Poniatowski as Lt. Col of the regiment 1770, (left center) Kazimerz Poniatowski from a portrait 1767-1773. (right) Figures based on Raspe.

General of the Crown Army under the Provisions of 17 July 1789.

(Left) A major general of the Grand Duchy based on Ignacy Morawski, 1789. (Left center) Major General of the Crown Army 1786 - 1788. (Right center) Major General 1789, (left) Major General in everyday dress 1785 - 1794.

(Left) A Major General in service dress wearing a "Jezefite" hat. The jacket is navy blue with crimson and silver. The cap is crimson with a blue band. Sash is silver with crimson threads. (Center) Kosciuszko in a pale coat, striped blue, red vest, white trousers with crimson and silver sash. (Right) Lt. General of the Grand Duchy. Crimson cap, navy jacket with collar, turnbacks and pants crimson. Epaulletes and embroidary yellow

Aide to General in German Dress, 1775. GNR

Adjutant to General in Polish Uniform, 1775. GNR

(Left) Lt. General based on a portrait of Jan Dabrowski in 1794. Crimson cap, Dark blue uniform, crimson facings. (Center) Kosciuszko in a black hat, white coat, navy blue pants with a crimson stripe. Navy holstr with crimson stripes based on Orlowski. (Right) a Major General of the Grand Duchy in 1794 based on Stachowicz. Navy blue uniform with crimson facings and gold lace. Silver/ Crimson sash.

(Left) Adjutant General in 1794 with crimson hat. Navy blue jacket with crimson faings and silver lace. Crimson pants with double silver stripes. The horse cloth is crimson with white and blue stripes. (Center) Kosciuszko orderly in 1794 - white cap, red band, green plume. White coat with red distinctions, black embroidery, pale vest. red/ silver sash, crimson pants with white stripe. (Right) Kosciuszko or commander of the Krakow battlaion - black hat, green feather, white coat with red collar and cuffs, and black embroidery. Navy pants with a crimson stripe.

Epaulettes of an ajdutant 1776 - 1780. MWPW

Epaulettes of an ajdutant 1776 - 1780. MWPW

Epaulettes of a lieutenant 1785 - 1795. MWPW

Army General of the Commonwealth of two Nations 1777 - 1794. MWPW

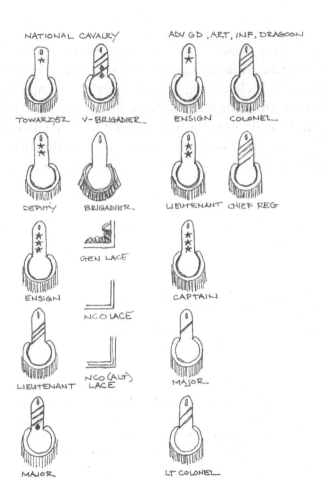

Officer Ranks 1770-1794. VR

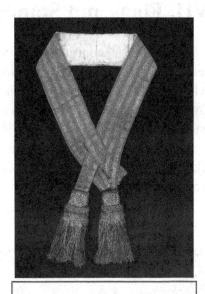

Officer sash 1789 - 1794. MWPW

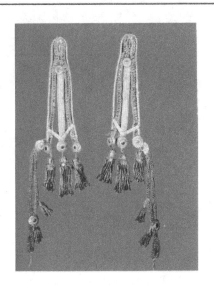

Epaullettes of the Chief of the Regiment 1764 - 1777. MWPW

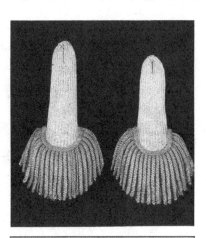

Officer epaullettes 1775. Jagiellonian University

VII. Flags and Standards

Flags, standards and guidons were used to indicate a unit – be it a company, squadron or regiment. During the Saxon period Polish-Lithuanian Infantry units adopted the Saxon regulation which would be a colored flag and a white flag. The colored flag was generally in the unit's color. By the end of the period the two flags might be a unit's flag and a national flag of the white Polish eagle on a crimson background. The regimental flag designs changed depending on the period.

Some units carried banners – which were flown horizontally rather than vertically, much like medieval troops. These could be seen amongst troops during the Bar Uprising and peasant troops.

The flag of Augustus II from 1702

Infantry banner of Stanislaw Leszczynski (1704 - 1736)in crimson silk, 175 cm x 255cm with yellow burgundy cross. A white eagle and gold crown. The staff was 175 cm long with a 21 cm leaf shapped tip. The reverse was the same.

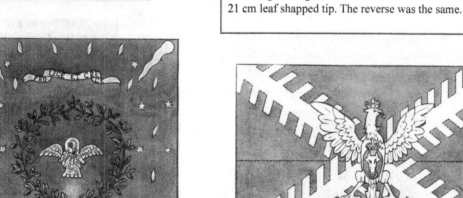

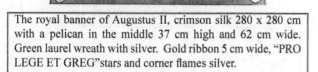

The royal banner of Augustus II, crimson silk 280 x 280 cm with a pelican in the middle 37 cm high and 62 cm wide. Green laurel wreath with silver. Gold ribbon 5 cm wide, "PRO LEGE ET GREG"stars and corner flames silver.

The banner of Adam Tarlo, a pancerni captain in 1731. A crimson field 215 cm x 260 cm. A white Polish cavalry cross on a yellow background 145 x 145 cm. The middle initials, "PG" (Gostynski District) are crimson sewn with black thread. The white letters up top, "PRO: FIDE: PATRIA: LEGE: et REGE". The corner is also white letters, "A.T.S.G.R.C.P." which stands for Adam, Starosta of Gsotynski Rotmistrz of the Pancenri Banner. The reverse is a mirror immage.	Cornet of the crown horse guards from the reign of Augustus II. Blue damask silk, 90 cm high, 93 cm wide and 70 cm in the middle.The initials and crown in silver. Green palm leaves and silver edging. The reverse similar.

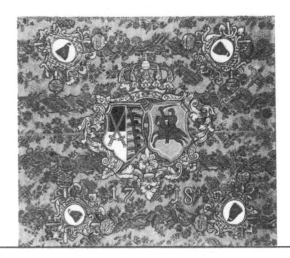

Banner of the foot guards of the crown under Augustus II. The background is white slk 178 cm x 227 cm. The center cartouches in the Rococo style The eagles and knight on a red background. The Saxon coat of arms below and a silver "AR" on a blue background. The cape is ermine with blue fabric 137 cm x 140 cm embroidered in gold and silver. The edges in crimson with yellow borders. The reverse is the same. The pole was painted black..	The banner of the 3rd Infantry - Field Hetman's Regiment - of the Grand Duchy in 1713 of Stanislaus Denhoff. It's field is green damask with the flowers slightly darker, 99 cm x 104cm. The two coats of arms are painted on - the Saxon and Lithuanian knight. The cartouche and crowns, and date is gold. The corners is the Denhoff coat of amrs.

The reverse side of the 3rd Infantry Regiment banner. The monogram, flames and inscriptions are painted in gold. The wording above the Virgin reads, "Sub Tuum Praesidium Confugimus". The initials in the monogram SDVDG stands for "Stanislaus Denhoff Vice Dux Generalis". He was Hetman from 1708 - 1728.

The banner of the Lithuanian Foot Guards from 1743. The background is white silk, 163 cm x 216 cm. The middle includes the Lithuanian Knight and the crown on a red background. On the corners are the monogram of the commander, "AC" for Augustus Czartoryski in red. The reverse is the same. Gembarzewski

The pennant for the artillery troops of the Grand Duchy at the time of Augustus II. The field is crimson silk, 72cm x 66cm x 47cm in the middle. In the middle of the left side is the Lithuanian Knight painted in oils 30 cm in diameter. The olive branches are green with a blue ribbon. The reverse has the cannon with a gold barrel and a red and white carriage. The pole was 99 cm in length painted blue, white and red. Gembarzewski

A banner of the artillery for the Army of Lithuania of crimson silk 142 cm x 215 cm with the middle circle being 44 cm diameter in white. The crown and monogram was gold with the initials A.P.R.G. - probably Anthony Pociej Commander Geneeral of Lithuania. Pociej was a supporter of Leszczynski in 1733. The reverse is similar except the cannon had a golden barrel and a red carriage.

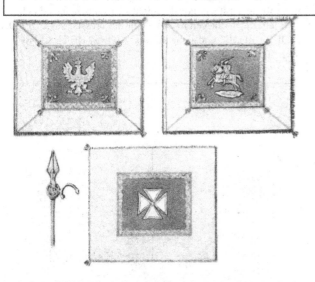

(Top) The penants of the royal escort. The background is crimson silk, 47 cm x 57 cm. The embroidered middle is 26 cm x 23 cm has a silver eagle. The frame and embroidery are silver. The center is a white damask belt 17 cm wide with crimson edging. The reverse had a Polish knight's cross in white 22 cm x 22 cm. The second penant was similar but with the Lithuanian Knight

(Left) Cavalry standard of 1764 of crimson damask, 70 cm x 70 cm. In the middle is a white eagle painted in oils. The initals SAR - Stanislaus Augustus Rex, in silver. The fringe is crimson.

The squadron coronets for the horse guards in blue with silver embroidery. The laurel leaves are green.

A banner of the Confederation of the Bar, 218 cm x 326 cm. The top is white and the bottom is crimson. The middle section is a 140 cm x 140 cm Polish Knight's Cross in reversed fields. The lettering is in yellow silk. On the cross it says, "PRO FIDE ET LEGE" and along the top, "MONSTRE TESSE MATREM".

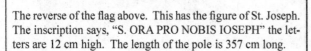

The reverse of the flag above. This has the figure of St. Joseph. The inscription says, "S. ORA PRO NOBIS IOSEPH" the letters are 12 cm high. The length of the pole is 357 cm long.

The flag of Confederate Karol Radziwiłł was white with red eagle, wreaths and initials. The Initials are "KR". The lettering around the figure of the madonna is gold, "MONSTRATE ESSE MATREM"

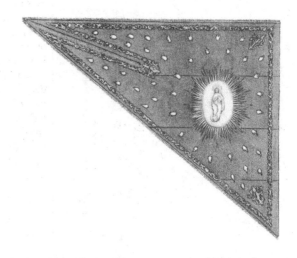

A banner of the Confederates of crimson silk 102 cm x 93 cm. The eagle is painted silver with a gold crown feet and beak. On the chest is a golden image of the Virign Mary holding a flaming heart. The eagle is 62 cm x 57 cm. Along the top is painted in silver, "SUB TUUM PRAESIDIUM CONFUGIMUS". On either side of the eagle are two white doves flying upward. The reverse is the same but the inscription says, "SUB UMBRA ALARUM TUARUM PROTEGE NOS. PS XCI".

Confederate banner of crimson silk, 185 cm along the pole and 226 cm on the fly. In the middel is the painted figure of the Virgin Mary of the Immactuate with golden rays. The painted flames moving from the Virgin Mary are yellow as is the fringe. The pole was painted yellow 297.5 cm long with a wooden tip.

A confederate banner illustrated and as an image. The banner is 212 cm x 147 cm painted on both sides. It depicts the leaders of the Bar Confederation Joseph Pulaski and Michael Krasinski. The other figures are idealized images of cossacks and Szlachta in friendship. The poles were painted blue and yellow 328 cm.

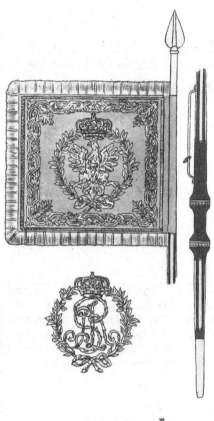

(Left) The banner of a National Cavalry squardon of crimson damsk 55 cm x 60 cm. The Eagle is silver 23.5 cm x 21 cm. The embroidery is silver with the initials SAR on the reverse. The spearhead is brass as is the butt plate. The pole is 290 cm painted black.

(right) the banner of the Crown Foot Guards of white silk, 140 cm x 155 cm. The embriodery is silver with the eagles gold and the riders in blue on red. The wreaths are greeen with blue and white ribbons. The reverse had silver initials SAR. The pole was 274 cm painted black. The battlaions banners would be in crimson.

Cornet of the crown horse guards in 1775. White damask silk, 86 cm x 93 cm to 53 cm in the middle. shield is red with golden thread seperating the quarters. The leaves in green and ribbon gold. SAR embroidered in silver. The pole was black, 305 cm long.

One of four Coronets of the Guard Cavalry in 1754, yellow silk 65 cm x 65 cm. Silver eagle with gold beak and sun. Embroidery silver on black ribbon, "TENDIT IN ARDU VIRTUS" On the reverse in silver is the monogram SARP and "PRO FIDE REGE LEGE ETLIBERTATE" pole is red 290 cm

The standard of the foot guards as shown on the previous page in the Polish Army Museum

Standard of a foot regiment with a crimson silk background, 136 cm high by 174 cm wide. Silver eagle with gold beak and legs, green laurels and light blue ribbon, 56 cm high x 60 cm wide. The reverse was the same with SAR in silver replacing the eagle.

(Right) Standard for a foot regiment of crimson silk, 154 cm high x 172 cm wide. The middle is embroidered silver 59 cm x 60 cm. The back was similar but the initials SAR replaced the eagle. The pole was painted black, 300 cm long.

The remnant of a green silk standard of 1794, 120 cm high x 125 cm wide. The eagle is painted white from oils with a gold crown. On the left side is "Wolnosc" and on the right "Calosc". The pole was black, 296 cm.

The banner of the 4th Infantry from 1794, 50 cm wide x 55 cm high and 36 cm in the middle. The words, "Niech Zyje Polska" in yellow silk above the eagle. Green fringe and yellow border. Gembarzewski lists the eagle as white, though it appears golden.

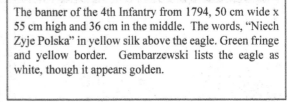

The standard of the Krakow Grenadier Battalion of scythemen. It is crimson silk, 128 cm high x 150 cm wide. The words, "ZYWIA Y BRONIA" embroidered in white silk.

A standard from the Kosciuszko period of crimson silk with the words, "WOLNOSC, CALOSC, NIEPOD-LEGOSC". The ribbon is crimson edged white.

The 2nd battalion standard of the 4th Regiment of the Crown Infantry, The Grand Hetman's Regiment, of yellow silk 100 cm high and 114 cm wide. All embroidery was silver thread.

Standard points from the Kosciuszko Uprising period.

VIII. Uniforms

Uniforms of Polish-Lithuanian Troops 1717 - 1764

A great source of uniforms of this period comes from a painting, "The Encampment of the Polish and Saxon Armies in 1732 at Warsaw" by Jan Christian Mock. The uniforms of the infantry following the Great Northern war took on the style and cut of Western Europe in general and the Saxon Army specifically. This consisted of knee length jackets with turnbacks showing the lining of the lapels, deep cuffs and skirts. Waistcoats and pants were the same color as the lining – which was the regimental color. Musketeers wore black tricornes with lace and grenadiers wore mitres or bearskins.

Cavalry contained a mixture of old styles to modern (for that era). Dragoons wore the uniform of the infantry, while hussars still wore armor (at least on parade) and would not have been out of place on the battlefield of Vienna until the 1730's. Eventually, the hussars and Advanced Guard units took on the look of what would become the more traditional lancer uniform.

Uniforms of the Barists

There was an attempt to uniform the cavalry in the old cavalry uniform of kontusz and zupan with an elongated konfederatka, but it quickly devolved into anything available. Infantry were often dressed in the colors of the noble who organized them such as Karol Radziwiłł. Eventually as foreign support came in some of the infantry were uniformed in white as the principal suppliers were Austria and France.

Uniforms of the Government 1764 - 1772

The Government forces consisted of infantry, cavalry and artillery for both the Kingdom of Poland and Lithuania organized along the lines of the Saxon army. For the infantry, the uniform was the long-tailed coat similar to all of Western Europe. The color, cuffs, lapels and turnbacks were of contrasting color to the coat and differentiated by regiments. The color of the infantry coat was red for Crown troops and blue for the Duchy. Cuffs and lapels were approximately 5 cm wide, and collar was about 5 cm high. The waistcoat was white or buff with color trim along the edges and pockets. Soldiers wore red or black cravats. Trousers were white with black thigh-high gaiters. Headgear consisted of a black tricorne for musketeers and brass plated mitre or bearskin for grenadiers and fusiliers. The tricornes had white lace. Swords had black leather scabbards with brass bindings.

Bar confederates - the soldiers in blue are based on figures appearing on Barist banner which were similar to Polish light cavalry. The soldier in red is based descriptions from the Lubelski Confederation.

The left figure is a cossack based on Morawski with a red kontusz, navy blue zupan and pants and a grey lambswool hat. Bar infantry in uniforms supplied by France or Austria. White uniforms with red turnbacks. Officer with silver lace.

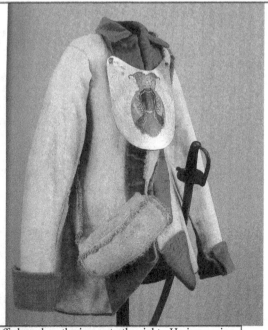

Barr cavlary - the figure on the left in a white jacket and red cuffs based on the image to the right. He is wearing crimson pants and yellow boots. The middle figure is wearing a pale jacket while the facings, zupan and pants are green and white stripes on the outside seam of the pants. The figure on the right is wearing a navy blue jacket while the turnbacks, zupan, pants and hat are crimson with yellow boots. MWPW

Details from the Monk picture in the 1730's. The top showing grenadiers and dragoons the the detail below showing fusiliers and musicians

In addition to musketeers there were Janissary and Hungarian companies in the King's Guard and the Hetman regiments. These were independent of the regimental structure. The Janissaries wore a hat called a Börk which consisted of a brass band with a plume holder. The hat was cylindrical felt with a white sleeve that hung down the back. By the late 18th century, the brass band extended upward into a stylized mitre/turban with a plume holder in front and the sleeve out the back. They also wore a long coat that tucked the ends into their belts.

Artillery for both countries during this period wore green jackets with black facings. The equipment was painted red with black metal works. For most part artillery pieces from this period were leftovers from the beginning of the century.

1770 Crown Infantry and Technical Corps

Commander	No.	Designation	Collar & Cuffs	Lapels	Buttons	Grenadiers
Czatoryski		Guards	Blue	Blue	Gold	Bearskins
Golcz	1	Queen Jadwiga	Black	Black	Silver	Bearskins
Witten	2	Crown Prince	White	White	Gold	Bearskins
Branicki	3	Grand Hetman	Green	Green	Gold	Brass Mitre
Branicki	4	Field Hetman	Light Blue	Light Blue	Silver	Bearskins
Potocki	5	Fusiliers	Black	Black	Gold	N/A
Sulkowski	6	Łanowy	Green	Green	Silver	Bearskin
Brühl		Artillery	Black	Black	Silver	N/A

1770 Crown Infantry - Independent Companies

Unit	Jacket	Trim	Facings	Pants	Hat
Grand Hetman Janissaries	Red	White	Green	Red	White
Grand Hetman Hungarian	Light Blue	Yellow	Red	Light Blue	Black
Field Hetman Hungarian	Light Blue	Yellow	Green	Light Blue	Black
Grand Marshal Hungarian	Blue	Silver	Orange	White	Brass Peaked
Warsaw Militia	Light Blue	Yellow	Light Blue	Light Blue	Black

An infantry officer from the 1770's from a painting by Canaletto

Cap plate of the Krasiński personal militia

Lithuanian Infantry from the 1770's. *GNR*

Cap plate of the Sanguszko personal militia

1770 Grand Duchy of Lithuania Infantry and Services

Commander	No.	Designation	Collar & Cuffs	Lapels	Buttons	Grenadiers
Czartoryski		Guard	Blue	Blue	Silver	Bearskin
Ogiński	1	Grand Hetman	White	White	Gold	Mitre
Sosnowski	2	Field Hetman	Black	Black	Gold	Black
Massalski		Artillery	Black	Black	Gold	Black
Cronenmann		Friekorps Artillery	Red	Red	Gold	Mitre

1770 Grand Duchy of Lithuania Infantry - Independent Companies

Unit	Jacket	Trim	Facings	Pants	Hat
Grand Hetman Janissaries	Red	Black	Black	Red	Red
Field Hetman Janissaries	Red	Green	Green	Red	Green
Grand Hetman Hungarian	Light Blue	Yellow	Yellow	Light Blue	Black
Field Hetman Hungarian	Light Blue	Yellow	Yellow	Light Blue	Black
Krejkompnie Art Grenadiers	Green	Red	Red	White	Mitre

The cavalry consisted of Hussars (heavy), Pancerni (medium) and light. Hussar companies wore a low *konfederatka* with white feathers, a crimson *kontusz* (a split sleeved coat) with blue facings and a blue *zupan* (a long-sleeved robe) beneath. They were armed with a lance, sabre and firearms. Some still wore breastplates. Pancerni companies wore these colors in reserve.

Light cavalry would be dressed in a felt or wool cap extending 6-8 inches high surrounded by a lambswool band. A *kontanka* (a short-sleeved jacket) was worn over a *zupan* and in contrasting colors to the *zupan*. These troops also carried a sabre, musket and light lance. The lance as 6-8 feet in length and surmounted by a swallowed tailed pennant that was divided horizontally.

Dragoons wore short infantry coats in green with regimental colors on the lapels, collars and cuffs. Boots were worn for mounted duty and gaiters for dismounted. In addition, they were armed with a sword, pistols and musketoon.

1770 Crown Cavalry

Commander	Designation	Kontusz	Facings	Zupan	Hat	Pennant
Poniatowski	Guard Dragoons	Buff	Red	-	Black	-
	Pancerni	Blue	Red	Red	Red	Blue/Red
	Hussars	Red	Blue	Blue	Blue	Red/Blue
Wojno	King's Lancers	Green	Crimson	-	Crimson	Red/Green / Red/Green
Raczynski	Podstoli Horse	Cornflower Blue	Yellow	Yellow	Light Blue	Blue/Yellow

1770 Crown Dragoons

Commander	Designation	Coat	Facings	Buttons	Lace
Poniatowski	Dragoon Guards	Buff	Red	Gold	White
Kozłowski	Queen's	Green	Red	Silver	White
Czapski	Prince's	Red	Green	Silver	White
Raczyński		Green	Red	Silver	White
Sułkowski		Green	Red	Silver	White
Branicki	Grand Hetman's	Green	Black	Silver	White
Rzewuski	Field Hetman's	Green	Red	Silver	White

1770 Grand Duchy of Lithuanian Cavalry

Commander	Designation	Kontusz	Facings	Zupan	Hat	Pennant
Grabowski	King's Horse Guards	Red	Blue	-	Black	-
	Petyhorski	Blue	Red	White	Blue	Blue/Red
Sapieha	Grand Hetman Light Horse	Green	Red	-	Red	Green/Red
Bielak	Potocki Tartars	Red	Yellow	-	Black	-
Poniatowski		White	Green	Green	Green	Red/Green

1770 Grand Duchy of Lithuania Dragoons

Commander	Designation	Coat	Facings	Buttons	Lace	Notes
Ogiński	King's	Green	Red	Gold	White	1775 – 5th Inf
Ogiński	Grand Hetman's	Green	Black	Gold	White	1775 – 2nd Inf
Sapieha	Field Hetman's	Green	Red	Gold	White	1775 – 4th Inf

All officers wore a sash that was red and silver. The knots are red and silver with fringe. These are tied on the right side. Shoulder straps for field officers are on the left side. Staff and general officers are on both shoulders. NCO's are distinguished by lace on the collar, cuffs and shoulder strap. Trumpeters have lace on the collars, cuffs and shoulders.

Uniforms 1772 - 1790

The infantry uniforms retained their style and color of Crown troops in red coats and Duchy troops in Blue. In 1789 the infantry were dressed in a blue *kurtka*, closed jacket with blue trousers for both the Crown and Grand Duchy. They were now wearing a shako with a tail at a time when King Stanislaw was trying to allow Polish troops to join in Russian operations against the Ottomans.

1776 Crown Infantry and Services

Commander	#	Designation	Collar & Cuffs	Lapels	Buttons	Grenadiers
Czartoryski		Guards	Blue	Blue	Gold	Bearskins
Golcz	1	Queen Jadwiga	Black	Black	Silver	Bearskin
Witten	2	Crown Prince	White	White	Silver	Bearskin
Branicki	3	Grand Hetman	Green	Green	Gold	Brass Mitre
Branicki	4	Field Hetman	Light Blue	Light Blue	Silver	Bearskin
Potocki	5	Fusiliers	Black	Black	Silver	N/A
Sulkowski, F	6	Łanowy	Green	Green	Silver	Bearskin
Raczyński	7	Cornflower	Blue	Cornflower Blue	Silver	Bearskin
Sułkowski, A	8	Ordynacja Rydzyńska	Yellow	Yellow	Silver	Brass Mitre
Lubirmirski	9	Grenadiers	Blue	Blue	Gold	Brass Mitre
Poniński	10		Apple Green	Apple Green	Gold	Bearskin
Granowski	11	Ostrogski Ordination	Black	Black	Gold	Brass Mitre
Brühl		Artillery	Black	Black	Gold	N/A
Klien		Engineers	Black	Black	Silver	N/A
Poninski		Pontoniers	Red	Red	Silver	N/A

1776 Crown Infantry Independent Companies

Unit	Jacket	Trim	Facings	Pants	Hat
Grand Hetman Janissary	Red	White	Green	Red	White
Grand Hetman Hungarian	Green	Yellow	Red	Green	Black
Field Hetman Hungarian	Red	Yellow	Green	Red	Black
Grand Marshal Hungarian	Blue	Silver	Orange	White	Fusilier Cap
Warsaw Militia	Light Blue	Yellow	Light Blue	Light Blue	Black

1776 Grand Duchy of Lithuania Infantry and Services

Commander	#	Designation	Collar & Cuffs	Lapels	Buttons	Grenadiers
Czartoryski		Guard	Blue	Blue	Gold	Bearskin
Oginski	1	Grand Hetman Grenadiers	White	White	Gold	Mitre
Oginski	2	Grand Hetman	Orange	Orange	Silver	Mitre
Sosnowski	3	Field Hetman	Black	Black	Gold	-
Sosnowski	4	Field Hetman	Red	Red	Silver	-
Grabowski	5	Grabowski	Yellow	Yellow	Silver	-
Massalski	6	Xavier Niesolowski	Crimson	Crimson	Silver	-
Stetkiewicz		Artillery	Black	Black	Gold	N/A

1776 Grand Duchy of Lithuania Independent Companies

Unit	Jacket	Trim	Facings	Pants	Hat
Grand Hetman Janissary	Red	Black	Black	Red	Red
Field Hetman Janissary	Red	Green	Green	Red	Green
Grand Hetman Hungarian	Light Blue	Yellow	Yellow	Light Blue	Black
Field Hetman Hungarian	Light Blue	Yellow	Yellow	Light Blue	Black

The ordinance of 9 February 1776 simplified the cavalry uniforms turning both hussars and pancerni cavalry into lancers. Horsemen were converted to expanded regiments known as national cavalry brigades. The former hussar banners wore crimson caps and *kontusz* with dark blue collars, cuffs and turnbacks. Crown troops had silver buttons and Lithuanian troops had gold buttons. The pancerni banners had navy *kontusz* and caps with crimson collars, cuffs and turnbacks - buttons as above. Under the *kontusz* they wore a long white *zupan*.

1776 Crown Cavalry

Commander	Designation	Kontusz	Facings	Zupan	Hat	Pennant
Poniatowski	Guard Dragoons	Buff	Red	-	Black	Red Talbard
Luba	1st Wielkopolska	Blue	Red	Red	Red	Blue/Red
Dzierżek	1st Ukrainian	Blue	Red	White	Red	Red with White Maltese cross
Zielonka	2nd Ukrainian	Light Blue	Crimson	White	Light Blue	Red with White Maltese cross
Lubowidzki	3rd Ukrainian	Blue	Red	Red	Blue	Blue/Red
Wojno	King's Lancer	Green	Red	-	Red	Green/Red
Byszewski	Adv Guard	Dark Blue	Red	Red	Red	Blue/Red
Kajetan	Adv Guard	Green	Black	Red	Green	Green/Black

1776 Crown Dragoons

Commander	Designation	Coat	Facings	Buttons	Lace	Notes
Kozłowski	Queen's	Green	Red	Silver	White	1st Adv Gd 1789
Branicki	Grand Hetman's	Green	Black	Silver	White	2nd Adv Gd 1789
Rzewuski	Field Hetman's	Green	Red	Silver	White	3rd Adv Gd - 1789
Raczynski		Green	Red	Silver	White	9th Inf - 1789
Czapski	Prince's	Red	Blue	Silver	White	8th Inf - 1789
Potocki		Green	Cornflower Blue	Silver	White	7th Inf - 1789

1776 Grand Duchy of Lithuania Cavalry

Commander	Designation	Kontusz	Facings	Zupan	Hat	Pennant
Grabowski	King's Horse Guards	Red	Blue	-	Black	-
Tyszkiewicz	Hussars of Kowienska	Dark Blue	Red	White	Red	Blue/Red
Chomiński	Petyhorski	Dark Blue	Yellow	White	Black	Blue/Yellow
Baranowski	1st Adv Guard	White	Yellow	Yellow	Yellow	Yellow/Lt Blue
Jeleński	2nd Adv Guard	White	Orange	Orange	Orange	Blue/Yellow
Romanowski	3rd Adv Guard	White	Blue	Blue	Blue	Blue/Yellow
Bielak	4th Adv Guard	White	Red	Red	Red	Red/Yellow
Hallaszewski	5th Adv Guard	White	Green	Green	Green	Yellow/Blue
Azulewicz	Tartars	Red	Yellow	-	Yellow	Red/Yellow

A drawing of National Cavalry uniforms based on the 1776 ordnances has the lance pennant fore Crown troops in crimson with a white Maltese cross centered toward the pole and Lithuania brigades with blue over the facing color.

Ordinance of 9 February 1778 changed the uniform style again. The national cavalry towarzysz had *konfederatkas* with red tops with a white band on top of a black lamb's wool band and a white plume. The jacket was a dark blue *kontusz* with crimson facings and a white vest. Some officers still wore a white *zupan*. The pants were crimson with a blue stripe down the side and on the cuffs. Troopers wore crimson belts. The shoulder cords and epaulette were silver as were the belt plates. The swords were black leather with brass bindings.

The troopers (*pocztowy*) wore blue jackets with blue pants. The collar, cuffs, facings, pant stripe and cuff were crimson. Their cap was a black mirliton, quilted shako or fur busby. The fur busby's could have red tops or bags. The cords were silver and crimson with white plume.

According to the provision of 27 February 1789 the advance guard units had a slightly different color scheme. The *towarzysz* wore a green kurtka with regimental facings and green trousers. The cap was a red konfederatka with a white base over black lamb's wool band. The cords were white with a white plume. The officer of the national cavalry wore a blue letwika with red cuffs, collar, shoulder strap and pants. The pants had a yellow side stripe. The belt was white and crimson.

The trumpeters wore scarlet kurtkas and pants with collar, lapels in navy blue. The pants stripe was white. The jacket lace along the back and sleeves were yellow. The collar and cuffs had silver lace. The plume was white with a blue top. The mirliton had white cords with a blue tassel at the end.

The saddle cloth was dark blue with the outer edge white (silver) with fringe, a red line, white, red and white. Silver eagles were in the hind corner at an angle with the eagles crown pointed toward the rider. The pistol holsters followed the same pattern with the king's initials in the center surmounted by a crown.

The dragoon regiments were eventually converted to infantry regiment or advanced guard units. Sometimes retaining their facing color and inserted into the regimental seniority.

Advanced guard units had blue or green jackets. Artillery continued to be clothed in green jackets with black facings, otherwise uniformed as infantry. From the Saxon monarchy period through the 1780's artillery equipment was painted red – the traditional Saxon color. The reform of 1788 changed the color of all equipment to green with black iron bands. As of 1792, there were still gun carriages in Częstochowa that were painted red and it was not fully changed over by the end of the period. The royal cypher was painted on it in white along with the unit number.

Uniforms 1791 - 1794

The Ordinance of March 1791 was the final re-organization of the army that eventually fought against Russia in defense of the Constitution. In the cavalry the height of konfederatka was lowered. In the National Cavalry Brigades the pocztowy was given a mirliton shako with a white plume and cords. The kurtkas were navy blue, with crimson distinctions - red pants with blue stripe.

In the Advance Guard pocztowy wore the same mirliton as in the National Cavalry Brigades with white over black plume. Towarzysz wore konfederatkas. Their kurtkas were green or blue. Collar and cuffs were black, lapels were crimson. The pants were crimson with black stripes. The buttons, lace and epaulettes were gold. The kiwer or mirliton at this period was black cylindrical, eight inches in height with a visor and neck guard.

The crown guard dragoons consisted of a round leather cap with a cloth turban, brass front plate which came to a point at the top. There was a leather peak surmounted by a horsehair mane and brass chinscales. The kurtka was red with blue distinctions and pants were blue with red stripes, but otherwise it was the new regulation style. The Lithuanian Guard cavalry seems to have retained the dragoon style bicorne but adjusted the rest of their uniform to the revised style.

Uniform of the National Cavalry (Polish Army Museum)

Detail of infantry from the Battle of Raclawice by Jan Matejko

Detail of Krakow Peasant Infantry at Raclawice from the Battle of Raclawice by Jan Matejko

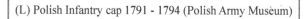

(R) Helmet of the Lithuanian Infantry 1791 - 1794 (Polish Army Museum)

(L) Polish Infantry cap 1791 - 1794 (Polish Army Museum)

1792 Crown Cavalry

Commander	#	Designation	Jacket	Facings	Buttons	Hat	Pennant
Potocki		Guard Dragoons	Red	Blue	Yellow	Black	-

NATIONAL CAVALRY

Commander	#	Designation	Jacket	Facings	Buttons	Hat	Pennant
Mioduski	1	1st Wielkopolska	Blue	Crimson	Silver	Crimson	Red/White Cross
Biernacki	2	2nd Wielkopolska	Blue	Crimson	Silver	Crimson	Red/White Cross
Hadziewicz	3	1st Malopolski	Blue	Crimson	Silver	Crimson	Red/White Cross
Manget	4	2nd Malopolski	Blue	Crimson	Silver	Crimson	Red/White Cross
Swiejkowski	5	3rd Ukrainian	Blue	Crimson	Silver	Crimson	Red Single Point
Jerlicz	6	2nd Ukrainian	Blue	Crimson	Red	Crimson	Red/White Cross
Lubowidzki	7	1st Ukrainian	Blue	Crimson	Red	Crimson	Red /White Cross
Sanguszko	8	4th Ukrainian	Blue	Red	Silver	Black	Red/White
Kening	1	King's Lancer	Green	Crimson	Gold	Crimson	Green/Red/Green/Red
	2	King's Lancers	Green	Black	Gold	Red	Green/Red

ADVANCED GUARD

Commander	#	Designation	Jacket	Facings	Buttons	Hat	Pennant
Szydłowski	1	Queen's	Blue	Crimson	Gold	Crimson	Crimson/Blue/White Fly/Crimson Maltese
Rzewuski	2		Green	Black	Gold	Red	Green/Black
Zajaczek	3		Dark Green	Blue	Gold	Dark Green	Green/Blue
Wurtemberg	4	Pr Wurtemberg	Blue	Red	Gold	Blue	Blue/Red
Lubormirski	5		Blue	Crimson	Gold	Crimson	Blue/Red

COSSACKS

Commander	#	Designation	Jacket	Facings	Buttons	Hat	Pennant
Potocki	1	Loyal Cossacks	Black	Red	-	Black	
Chomentowski	2	Loyal Cossacks	Black	White	-	Red	

1792 Grand Duchy of Lithuania Cavalry

Commander	#	Designation	Jacket	Facings	Buttons	Hat	Pennant
Stryjennki		Horse Guards	Red	Blue	Gold	Black	

NATIONAL CAVALRY

Commander	#	Designation	Jacket	Facings	Buttons	Hat	Pennant
Ostrowski	1	Hussars of Kowiensk	Blue	Crimson	Gold	Crimson	Blue/Red
Twardowski	2	Light Horse of Pinsk	Blue	Crimson	Gold	Crimson	Blue/Yellow
Kossakowski	3		Blue	Crimson	Gold	Crimson	Blue/Red

ADVANCED GUARD

Commander	#	Designation	Jacket	Facings	Buttons	Hat	Pennant
Kirkor	1		Blue	Red	Gold	Red	Blue/Red
Jeleński	2		Blue	Red	Gold	Red	Blue/Red
Chlewiński	3		Blue	Red	Gold	Red	Blue/Red
Bielak	4	Jozef Bielak	Blue	Red	Gold	Red	Blue/Red
Byszewski	5	Stan. Byszewski	Blue	Red	Gold	Red	Blue/Red
Azulewicz	6	2nd Nadworina Ulan	Red	Yellow	Silver	Red	Red/Yellow
Ulan	7	Tartars	Red	Yellow	Silver	Red	Red/Yellow

In 1791 a shako (also called a *kasziet* in Polish) was introduced for the Polish Infantry units. It had a low crown with a white metal front plate, plume on the left side and a crest that went from back to front. This incorporated elements of design similar to shakos worn in the Austrian, Prussian and Russian armies, but was uniquely Polish in its final form.

For Lithuanian troops a helmet was introduced similar to the rumplehelm. It consisted of a helmet 8-10 inches tall with a rounded top made of black felt. A plate of the Lithuanian horseman or Polish Eagle was fixed to the front on a brass band. On an existing copy in the Polish Army museum there are fold up flaps on the back and side and the words "Rex et Patria" on the band. A black bearskin crest went from the back' halfway up the top.

1792 Crown Infantry and Services

Commander	#	Designation	Collar & Cuffs	Lapels	Buttons
Poniatowski		Guards	Blue	Blue	Gold
Gorzeński	1	Queen Jadwiga	Crimson	Crimson	Gold
Wodzicki	2	Crown Prince	Crimson	Crimson	Silver
Czapski	3	King's	Green	Green	Silver
Branicki	4	Field Hetman	Green	Green	Silver
Rzewuski	5	Fusiliers	Black	Black	Gold
Ożarowski	6	Łanowy	Forrest Green	Forrest Green	Gold
Potocki	7		Cornflower Blue	Cornflower Blue	Gold
Rzewuski	8	Grand Hetman	Light Blue	Light Blue	Silver
Raczynski	9		Pink	Pink	Silver
Dzialyński	10		Yellow	Yellow	Gold
Illiński	11	Grenadiers	Yellow	Yellow	Gold
Lubormirski	12		Apple Green	Apple Green	Silver
Poninski	13	Ostrogski Ordination	Yellow	Yellow	Gold
Potocki	14		Light Blue	Light Blue	Silver
Cichocki	15		Black	Black	Gold
		Krakow Garrison	Black	Black	Silver
Wierzbowski		Czestochowa Garrison	Black	Black	Silver
Potocki		Artillery	Black	Black	Gold
Potocki		Engineers	Black	Black	Silver
Kossowski		Pontoneers	Red	Red	Silver

1792 Grand Duchy of Lithuania Infantry and Services

Commander	#	Designation	Collar & Cuffs	Lapels	Buttons
Jabłonowski		Guard	Blue	Blue	Silver
Oginski	1	Grand Hetman Grenadiers	Red	Red	Gold
Oginski	2	Grand Hetman	Orange	Orange	Silver
Tyszkiewicz	3	Field Hetman	Green	Green	Gold
Judycki	4	Field Hetman	Tourquoise	Tourquoise	Silver
Grabowski	5	Grabowski	Light Blue	Light Blue	Silver
Niesiołowski	6	Xavier Niesolowski	Yellow	Yellow	Silver
Sapieha	7	Prince Sapieha	Black	Black	Silver
Rzewuski	8	Radziwill Infantry	Black	Black	Silver
Radziwiłł	9		Black	Black	Silver
Kosielski		Artillery	Black	Black	Gold

1792 Grand Duchy of Lithuania Infantry Independent Companies

Unit	Jacket	Trim	Facings	Pants	Hat
Grand Hetman Hungarian	Light Blue	Yellow	Yellow	Light Blue	Black
Field Hetman Hungarian	Light Blue	Yellow	Yellow	Light Blue	Black

Prior to 1792 and after 1794 Polish infantry regiments contained a grenadier component, but regulations from the era seem silent on them. It would be logical that they were still an organic part of the regiment and denoted by the sideways crest (as Prussian and Russian grenadiers had during this period). Some troops within units are shown with sideways crests in white in the iconography of the period, but the illustrations are silent in their description.

For artillery, engineers and pontoniers they wore green kurtkas with the facing color of their branch and the headgear of the respective army.

1794 Crown Infantry and Services

Commander	#	Designation	Collar & Cuffs	Lapels	Buttons
Poniatowski		Guards	Blue	Blue	Gold
Gorzenski	1	Queen Jadwiga	Pink	Pink	Gold
Wodzicki	2	Crown Prince	Pink	Pink	Silver
Czapski	3	Junior King	Green	Green	Silver
Branicki	4	Field Hetman	Green	Green	Silver
Rzewuski	5	Fusiliers	Black	Black	Gold
Ozarowski	6	Lanowy	Forrest Green	Forrest Green	Gold
Potocki	7		Cornflower Blue	Cornflower Blue	Gold
Rzewuski	8	Grand Hetman	*Passed into Russian service – Kamienets Musketeer Regiment*		
Raczynski	9		Pink	Pink	Silver
Dzialynski	10		Yellow	Yellow	Gold
Illinski	11	Grenadiers	*Passed into Russian Service Mohylewski Musketeer Regiment*		
Lubormirski	12		*Passed into Russian Service as Izialav Grenadier Regiment*		
Poninski	13	Ostrogski Ordination	Yellow	Yellow	Gold
Potocki	14		*DISBANDED*		
Cichocki	15		Black	Black	Gold
Gisiler	16	Treasury	Black	Black	Gold
Rottenburg	17		Black	Black	Gold
Krasiński	18		Black	Black	Gold
Sokolnicki	19	Riflemen	Green	Green	Silver
Kiliński	20		Red	Red	Gold
Paszkowski	21	Podlaski Pikemen	Black	Black	Gold
		Krakow Garrison	Black	Black	Silver
		Volunteer Infantry	Yellow	Yellow	Silver

Commander	#	Designation	Collar & Cuffs	Lapels	Buttons
Potocki		Artillery	Black	Black	Gold
Potocki		Engineers	Black	Black	Silver
Kossoski		Pontoniers	Red	Red	Silver

A scene from the Raclawice Pararama showing Polish 2nd infantry firing on Russian Cavalry.

The cap proportedly that of Thaddeus Kosciuszko from 1794. PAM

Buttons recovered from the Zielence battlefield from the 11th, 13th and 12th regiments. Oleg Pogorelec

1794 Grand Duchy of Lithuania Infantry and Services

Commander	#	Designation	Collar & Cuffs	Lapels	Buttons
Jablonowski		Guard	Blue	Blue	Silver
Oginski	1	Grand Hetman	Red	Red	Gold
Oginski	2	Grand Hetman	Orange	Orange	Silver
Tyskiewicz	3	Field Hetman	Green	Green	Gold
Judycki	4	Field Hetman	Turquoise	Turquoise	Silver
Grabowski	5	Grabowski	Light Blue	Light Blue	Silver
Niesiolowski	6	Xavier Niesolowski	Yellow	Yellow	Silver
Sapieha	7	Prince Sapieha	Black	Black	Silver
Radziwill	8	Radziwill Infantry	Black	Black	Silver
Radziwill	9		Black	Black	Silver
Kosielski		Artillery	Black	Black	Gold
Sapieha		Engineers	Black	Black	Gold

Soldiers from the Kościuszko Uprising by Stachowicz.
From left to right, two cavalry officers, a soldier from
the Hetman's Regiment, a sharpshooter from Wodzicki's
regiment and an officer from Capski's

1794 Crown Cavalry

Commander	#	Designation	Jacket	Facings	Buttons	Hat	Pennant
Potocki		Guard Dragoons	Red	Blue	Yellow	Black	-

NATIONAL CAVALRY

Commander	#	Designation	Jacket	Facings	Buttons	Hat	Pennant
Madaliński	1	1st Wielkopolska	Blue	Crimson	Silver	Crimson	Red/White Cross
Biernacki	2	2nd Wielkopolska	Blue	Crimson	Silver	Crimson	Red/White Cross
Hadziewicz	3	1st Malopolski	Blue	Crimson	Silver	Crimson	Red/White Cross
Manget	4	2nd Malopolski	Blue	Crimson	Silver	Crimson	Red/White Cross
Świejkowski	5	3rd Ukrainian	*Passed to Russian Service – Dniepiski Brigade*				
	6	2nd Ukrainian	*Passed to Russian Service – Dniestrzanski Brigade*				
Lubowidzki	7	1st Ukrainian	*Passed to Russian Service – Braclawski Brigade*				
	8	4th Ukrainian	*Disbanded*				
Wojciechowski		King's Lancer	Green	Crimson	Gold	Crimson	Green/Red

ADVANCE GUARD

Commander	#	Designation	Jacket	Facings	Buttons	Hat	Pennant
Szydłowski	1	Queen's Adv Gd	Green	Crimson	Gold	Crimson	Crimson/Blue/White Fly, Crimson Maltese
	2	Advance Guard	*Passed to Russian Service - Zytomirski Regiment*				
Zajaczek	3	Advance Guard	Blue	Crimson	Gold	Crimson	Red/White/Red/White
Byszewski	4	Advance Guard	*Passed to Russian Service – Konstantynowki Regiment*				
Lubormirski	5	Advance Guard	*Passed to Russian Service - Iziastanski Regiment*				
Joselwicz		Starozakonna Light Cavalry	Black	-	Silver	Black	
Krasicki		Hussars	Blue	Yellow	Gold	Black	

1794 Grand Duchy of Lithuania Cavalry

Commander	#	Designation	Jacket	Facings	Buttons	Hat	Pennant
Stryjeński		Horse Guards	Red	Blue	Gold	Black	

NATIONAL CAVALRY

Commander	#	Designation	Jacket	Facings	Buttons	Hat	Pennant
Ostrowski	1	Hussars of Kowiensk	Blue	Crimson	Gold	Crimson	Blue/Red
Twardowski	2	Light Horse of Pinsk	Blue	Crimson	Gold	Crimson	Blue/Yellow
Kossalowski	3		Blue	Crimson	Gold	Crimson	Blue/Red

ADVANCED GUARD

Commander	#	Designation	Jacket	Facings	Buttons	Hat	Pennant
Kirkor	1	*Lithuanian-Tartar Regiment Russian Army 1793*					
Kadłubiński	2		Blue	Red	Gold	Red	Blue/Red
Piruski	3		Blue	Red	Gold	Red	Blue/Red
Bielak	4	Jozef Bielak	Blue	Red	Gold	Red	Blue/Red
Lissowski	5	Stan. Byszewski	Blue	Red	Gold	Red	Blue/Red
Achmatowicz	6	2nd Nadworina Ulan	Blue	Red	Gold	Red	Red/Yellow
Ulan	7	Tartars	Navy	Red	Silver	Red	Red/Blue
Weyssenhoff	8		Blue	Red	Gold	Red	Blue/Red

Note: Even though some units were incorporated into the Russian Army, the Polish command tried to raised new troops to fill those regiment numbers. They would have been uniformed as the predecessors.

Targowica Confederation 1792

CAVALRY

Commander	Designation	Jacket	Facings	Hat	Pennant
Borzęcki	Kiev Hussars	Blue	Crimson	Crimson	Blue/Red
Zlotnicki	Podolska Golden Freedom	Blue	Crimson	Crimson	Blue/Red
Suchorzewski	Braclawice Hussars	Blue	Crimson	Crimson	Blue/Red
Potocki	Humanski Light Cavalry	Blue	Crimson	Crimson	Blue/Red
Leszczyński	Free Federation Ad. Guard	Blue	Crimson	Crimson	Blue/Red

INFANTRY

Commander	Designation	Jacket	Facings	Hat
Moszczewski	Infantry	Blue	Yellow	Blue

IX. The Units of the Armies of Poland and the Grand Duchy of Lithuania 1707 – 1795

(Note: this list is not exclusive, but represents the units we have identified with commanders and uniforms)

The units had a "Chief" who was the units nominal commander but was commanded in the field by its colonel

Crown Infantry

Foot Guard Regiment of the Crown

The guard regiment was one of the oldest units in the army and was stationed in Warsaw. It was originally titled the Das Hochlöbliche Königliche Polnische Kron-Guardes Infanterie Regiment – reflecting the German nature of the Crown during the early 18th century.

Garrisoned: Warsaw

Chiefs: Fieldmarshal Jakób Henry Flemming 1717-1732; Prince August Czartoryski Lt. Gen in the Russian Army. 1732 until his death on 4.IV.1782; Prince Stanisław Poniatowski, Swordbearer of the Grand Duchy of Lithuania, Lt. Gen of the Crown Army 1782 – 1789; Prince Józef Poniatowski 1789 – 1792; Piotr Ożarowski, Crown Grand Hetman 1793.

Colonels: Gen. Grzegorzewski 1717; Prince August Czartoryski 1 Apr 1729, Maj. Gen. 14.June 1762; Maj. Gen. Karol Ernest Coccei, 22 Apr 1767 until his death 1782; August Ulmitz 28 May 1782, Hiż Du Laurans 31 Dec 1783; Ludwig Dahlke 1792; Trzciński 1794.

The infantry fought at Warsaw and its environs, Powązki, Górce, Zegrze, Powązki, Karczma Welański, Krupczyce, Brześć, Maciejowice and Praga during the Kosciuszko Revolt

Crown Foot Guards of the 1730's

(Left) winter clothing 1765. (center) A Grenadier in summer dress. (Right) A staff officer suggested to be The head of the regiment, August Czartoryski.

Musicians of the guard in the 1730's, which included a sapper company. The jackets are yellow, the zupan, pants and hat are light blue. Boots are yellow. The lace is white. Sapper cap has brass fittings. Goat bagpipies are white with silver.

The foot guards in 1770 based on Canaletto. The officer on horseback has a red uniform with blue facings, black hat with gold braid and gold buttons. The center officer is from 1778 Same as previous, but bow is white, epaulets gold, sash silver with red. The grenadiers bearskin is black with a brass plate - back of cap is blue.

Guard infantry in the summer uniform, 1792. JH

109

(Top Left) Jozef Poniatowski as Szef of the regiment in 1792 based on an image by Bacciarelli as well as another view of a grenadier in the summer uniform.

(Top Right) The foot guards in 1794, the soldier wears a red kurtka with dark blue turnbacks and trousers. The hungarian knots on the pants is yellow. Cap plate is brass with a silver eagle. The commanders helmet was brass with a leopard turban. Sash is silver with red.

(Left) Another view of the guard in 1794 based on paintings by Orlowski.

Miscellaneous Guard Units

In addition to Guard regiments, which could operate in the field, there were also personal guard units that guarded the King in his daily life. These were smaller units termed "companies" but probably never numbered more than 100 men for each unit. Some had their origin story back in the history of medieval or renaissance Poland while others like the Janissaries were of more recent origins. But because they were the guards of the king, they were dressed in more impressive, albeit impractical military dress, meant to impress rather than function.

(Top Left) Guard Musketeers from 1729 to 1735. on the left is a soldier, the middle a lieutenant and the right a captain. the oversized bandelier was a remnant of an earlier era.

(Top Right) Hajduks based on the encampment of the Polish and Saxon troops near Warsaw, by Monk in 1732 are on the left. The central figure is based on Canaletto from the election of Poniatowski in 1764 as are the figures on the right.

(Left) A hussar with a light brown cap and red bag. A light green doman and pants, blue braiding. Red and green belt, Red pelisse. (Right) red dolman and pants with blue pelisse, white braid and grey fur. Cap was red with blue band.

Janissaries of the guard of the king on the left and the kolpack and sword on the right. Most likely this was uniformed in red and yellow like the musketeers.

An officers and a towarzysz of the royal escort squadron based on a 1770 painting by Canaletto. The front right figure is identified as a general in the uniform of a pre-reform Hussar.

(Left) The King's Mounted Rifles. Black hat with gold braid, green coat with pale turnbacks, pale torusers and gold braid from 1768. (Right) A Hajduk of the King based on his servant who died defending the king in 1771. The dolman is white, blue and gold lace. Crimson pants, yellow shoes, black hat with gold braid. The girdle and sabetache are gold.

1ˢᵗ *Foot Regiment of the Crown*

This was one of the oldest regiments in the army after the foot guards. King Stanisłaus Augustus named it after his patron Queen Jadwiga.

During this period the units was stationed in Poznań (1775), Kalisz (1785), Winnica (1788), Piotrków (1789), Stary Konstantynów (1791), Kalisz and Pleszew in October 1792 and Parczew and its vicinity in 1793.

Chiefs: The Honorable Joachim Fryderyk Flemming, Lt. Gen. of the Saxon Army, Treasurer of Lithuania 1717 – 1763; August Stanisław Golcz, 21 Mar 1763, Maj. Gen as of18.XII.1777; Samuel Ożarowski 13 Mar 1780; Lt. Gen. August Gorzeński 24 Feb 1790; Antoni Puławski, Inspector General of the Crown Armies 1793 – 1794.

Colonels: Józef Biernacki; Maj. Gen. Karol Ludwik de Fiszer 4 Nov 1771; Hoffman Ignacy Szeński, 13 Nov 1783; Lt. Col. Kurcyusz May 1791; Jan Grochowski Jan 1792, Maj Gen from. Apr 1794, died 6.June.

Battles and Skirmishes: Confederation of the Bar, Piotrków, Skrzynno, Zbąszyn. **1792** Boruszkowce 15 June, Zieleńce 17 June, Dubienka 18 July, Zasław. **1794** Szczekociny 6 June, around Warsaw, Powązki 28 July.

1732 - Officer and Grenadier

1732 - NCO with a partizan and a lieutenant holding a standard

Grenadier mitre 1st reg 1770-89

(Left) Officer in 1763, (middle) solider, 1775 (right) NCO in summer uniform 1787

Officer and soldier, 1775 GNR

Musketeer in 1789 regulation dress.

(Left) Officer in summer dress 1794, (mid) regimental commander Augustus Gorzenski, (right) Soldier.

2nd Foot Regiment of the Crown

This regiment was founded by Augustus III in the name of his third son Karol. It retained the numeral 2 in the hierarchy until the end of the Kosciuszko Insurrection.

The Regiment of His Majesty Prince Frederick (1748 – 1764), commonly known as the Saxon or Crown Prince Regiment.

Garrisoned: Kamieniec, Poznań, Kraków from 1775.

Chief: Dönhof, Gen. of the Lithuanian Artillery 1717 – 1737; Leon Raczyński 1737; Lt. Gen. Jerzy Wilhielm Goltz Jerzy 1737 till his death in 24 Apr 1767; Maj. Gen. Karol Wojciech Szak, Baron of Wittenow. 6 Apr1763; Józef Wodzicki, Adj. Gen to his Majesty 4 Feb1782.

Colonels: Flemming 1718; Maj. Gen. Jan Krzysztof de Bardeleben, died 1748, August Stanisław Goltz., brother of the chief, 20 July 1748, a Maj. Gen July 1758, to the King's Regiment 21 Mar 1763; Stefan Sułkowski 1763; Jan Jakób Dawid von Grammlich 24 Mar 1766; Adam Heppen 1789.

Battles and Skirimishes: Confederation of the Bar, Bydgoszcz, Chodzież, Kościan, Starogród, Piotrków 1768, Skrzynno 9 Apr 1769. **1792** Granne 24 July **1794** Racławice 4 Apr, Szczekociny 6 June, around Warszawy, Szczęśliwice 17 and 18 Aug, Maciejowice 10 Oct, Radoszyce 18 Nov.

Two battalions of the unit took part in the Battle of Racławice including a company of riflemen.

(Left) The regimental commander in 1763, (center) soldier in 1775, (right) grenadier from the same period.

(Left) Adjutant to the Commander 1789 - 91, (Left-center) staff officer in parade dress, (right-center) soldier in summer dress 1790 - 91, (right) private in parade dress.

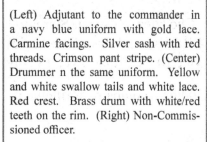

(Left) Adjutant to the commander in a navy blue uniform with gold lace. Carmine facings. Silver sash with red threads. Crimson pant stripe. (Center) Drummer n the same uniform. Yellow and white swallow tails and white lace. Red crest. Brass drum with white/red teeth on the rim. (Right) Non-Commissioned officer.

Soldiers at the time of the Kosciuszko Uprising (1794) MS

3rd Foot Regiment Czapski

This unit was originally called the Prince's Dragoon Regiment, formed in 1776. When inserted into the line infantry in 1789 it was originally numbered eight, but in 1790 the Colonel-in-Chief Mikołaj Czapski had it moved to number three – which it remained during the hostilities of 1792 and 1794.

The regiment also went by the names King's Junior Regiment and Czapski's Grenadier Regiment.

Garrisoned: Łowicz, Józefów (1777), Radom, Kielce 1789, Kraków 1794.

Chief: Lt Gen. Antoni Czapski Ant., 1776, Maj Gen. Mikołaj Czapski 1787, died. 20VII.1792

Colonels: Karol Mannstejn, 1776; Mikołaj Czapski (1785); Józef Czapski 1787; Jazoszewski (1794); Krzycki, killed 4 Nov 1794.

Battles and Skirmishes: **1792** Zieleńce 17 June, Dubnika 7 July, Dubienka 18 July; **1794** Racławice 4 Apr, Szczekociny 6 June, Maciejowice 10 Oct, Praga 4 Nov.

Two battalions of the regiment plus riflemen took part in the battle of Racławice.

1791 - 1794 Drummer had blue jackets, white "v" lace on the sleeves. The drummer's helmet had a red crest. The drum was brass; the border had red and white teeth on the borders. Soldiers had red distinctions and side stripes. The rank and file wore white leatherwork. The officers had silver epaulettes.

The sharpshooters wore a black broad brimmed hat with a green plume. They wore the regulation jacket and pants with black belts. Stachowicz shows the riflemen in blue rather than green uniforms with yellow pants stripes. The leatherwork for the riflemen was black per regulation. Hat plume was white

(Left) A staff officer 1791 - 94. (Center) A line officer 1789 - 91. (Right) Officer at the Lublin garrison in 1793.

(Left) Drummer with red crest, lace is white. Rim of the brass drum with red and white teeth. (Center) Soldier, (right) Sharpshooter with a green feather

Soldiers of the 3rd regiment at the time of the Kosciuszko Uprising (1794) MS

4th Foot Regiment Grand Hetman of the Crown

It was formed in 1726, becoming the Crown Grand Hetman's Regiment in 1752, it received the number designation 1789. It was originally designated number 3, and then redesignated number 4 in 1790 where it remained during the rest of its existence.

Garrisoned: Białystok, Lwów 1771, Kamieniec (1775), Łęczna 1778, part in Małopolska June 1789, Białocerkiew, part in Ukraińe-Podolska, Nov, part Wołyńska, Lubomia 1794.

Chiefs: Adam Mikołaj Sieniawski, Crown Grand Hetman 30 Apr 1706, died 18 Feb 1726; Stanisław Chomętowski, Crown Grand Hetman 11 Oct 1726, died 2 Sept 1728; Gryf Jan Klemens Branicki., Crown Grand Hetman 1735, w. kor. 5 June 1752, died 9 Oct 1771; within a year and a half, Wacław Rzewuski 9 Apr 1773 to 16 Feb1774; Franczusek Ksawery Branicki of the arms Korczak 8 Feb 1774 do 1793.

Colonels: Gen. Barącz 1718; Maj Gen. Kamiński (1750-1762); Maj. Gen. Bernard de Pugget (1767); Maj. Gen. Felicjan Korytowski, 1 July 1770 – (1790); Karwowski 25 May 1790; Karol Morawski 1792; Capt Poklękowski.

Battles and Skirmishes:1792 Zieleńce 17 June, Dubniki 7 July; **1794** Szczekociny 6 July, Wawrzyszew 26 Aug, Bielany 1 Sept, Praga 4 Nov.

The Grand Hetman Regiment in 1713. (Left) Drummer in reverse colors. (Center) Grenadier in low cap. (Right) NCO with a polearm.

The Grand Hetman Regiment in 1732. Officers of the Grenadiers based on Mock.

The Grand Hetman Regiment in 1775. (Left) musketeer, (center) staff officer, (right) grenadier in brass miter.

The 4th Regiment in 1791. (Left) soldier in greatcoat. (Left-center) Soldier on the march. (Right-center) NCO in parade dress. (Right) Soldier in summer dress.

4th Regiment 1794. MS

5th *Regiment of Fusiliers*

The tradition of this regiment claims its foundation during the Vienna Campaign under Jan Sobieski. The Sejm of 1717 numbered this regiment as number five in the army's hierarchy under the king. The nominal chief of the regiment was taken over by the General of Artillery of the Crown.

The 18th century the regiment supported the artillery and was known as the Fusilier regiment. In 1775 the name was changed from, "The Fusilier Regiment of the Crown Artillery"" to the Fusilier Battalion. In 1776 it was listed in the army as the 5th Regiment of Fusiliers. In 1789 it returned to its original name. In 1788 it was re-numbered in the hierarchy to number six. In 1792 it returned to being number five.

Garrisoned: Kamieniec Podolski, Białystok 1776, Warsaw.

Chiefs: Gen of Artillery Rybiński, Governor of Chełm 1717 – 1725; Kącki, Swordbearer kor. 1725 – 1732; Jan Klemens Branicki 1732 – 1739; Adolf Rybiński 1739 – 1749; Prince Lubomirski 1749 – 1753; The Honorable Ocieszyna Brühl, Starosta of Spis, First Minister 1753, The Honorable Aloizy Fryderyk Brühl, Gen. of Artillery, Starosta of Spis 1762; Stanisław Szczęsny Potocki, Gen of Artillery 1791; Rzewuski, Crown Secretary until 1 Aug 1792; Gen. Wielhorski 1 Aug 1792, Gen. of Artillery Potocki 1793.

Colonels: Florjan Szyling 1717; Lt. Gen Józef Rottermund (1762) died 18 Mar 1774; Mycielski 1774; Col. Jan August Cichocki 1778, Maj. Gen. 1790, vacant. Jan Fontana 1794.

Battles and Skirmishes: **1792** Boruszkowce 15 June; Zieleńce 17 June; Włodzimierz 7 July; Dubienka 18 July; **1794** The Warsaw Uprising 17 June; Chełm 8 June, Słonim 1 Aug, Krupczyce 16 Sept, Maciejowice 10 Oct, Praga 4 Nov.

In the Kosciuszko Insurrection two companies were stationed in Warsaw, the rest of the regiment was stationed in Chełm (4 April 1794).

The sharpshooters wore a light green uniform with black distinctions, but with white leatherwork. They wore black half boots and pants had black side stripes. They had black round hats.

Fusiliers in 1752. Red coat, pants, vest and turnbacks. Black hat with white lace and bow.

Fusiliers in 1775 - fusilier (left) and officer (right)

Fusiliers 1791 - 1794.

6th *Foot Regiment of* Łanowy

The regiment has its origins in 1726 with the Łanowy (King's landed peasantry) regiment which traditionally had been associated with the Crown Estates Militia. It was originally called the Guard Łanowy (Gwardia Łanowa) and designated as number six. For a short time in 1790 it was number nine and in 1791 it was number seven. Finally in 1792 it returned to number six.

The Unit was formed in 1726.

Garrisoned: Kamieniec Podolski, Wschowa, Warsaw 1775, Part in Wielkopolska, Wschowa 1779, Włodzimierz 1790, Wolbrom 1790, Wschowa X.1792

Chiefs: Jan Klemens Branicki 1726, Governor of Lublin, Lt. Gen in 1729; Maj. Antoni Kossowski, Court Treasurer; Prince Franciuszek Sułkowski. Inspector of the Infantry 1 Sept 1775; Jan Fryderyk Brodowski 11 May 1789 – 1793, Hetman Stanisław Ożarowski 1793 – 1794.

Colonels: Jan Rosen (1764), Łuba (1774), Wojciech Dąbkowski (1776), Józef Jankowski until 1778, Józef Laskowski until 1781, Jan Gotfried de Suessmilch (1786), Jan Fryderyk Brodowski 1787 do 12.V. 1789, Maciej Szyrer (1789), M Zawisza. 1793.

Battles and Skirmishes: **1792** Zieleńce 17 June, Opalin 13 July; **1794** Racławice 4 Apr, Szczekociny 6 June, Around Warsaw, Praga 4 Nov.

6th Foot - Lanowy Regiment

Top Left: 1732, Regimental chief on the horse. Officer of the musketeers, officer of the Grenadiers and a grenadier. Taken from Mock.

Top Right: 1775, Officer and musketeer based on Raspe

Bottom left: 1791 - 1794 - private

7th Foot Regiment Potocki

The regiment was founded in 1776 as a dismounted dragoon regiment. In 1789 it was converted into an infantry regiment, "Infantry Regiment of Colonel Potocki, Starosta of Szczerzec" under the control of Piotr Franciszek Potocki and received number 7. It was later involved in the Targowica Confederation.

The unit was originally numbered number seven. In the years 1790-1794 it moved around – in 1790- 1792 it was number eight, in 1792 it was number nine and during the Kosciuszko Insurrection it was returned to number seven. The regiment took part in the War in Defense of the Constitution.

Garrisoned: Kalisz, Poznań 1786, Łowicz 1790

Chiefs: Jan Potocki, Starosta of Szczyrzycki 1776; Piotr Francuszek Potocki, Starosta of Szczyrzycki 28.X.1778; Miączyński, Secretary pol. of the Crown 1793

Colonels: Robert de Tayler (1780 – 1787), Michał Zawisza (1789) – 1794.

Battles and Skirmishes: 1792 Zieleńce 17 Apr; **1794** Szczekociny 6 June, Raszyn June, Gołków 9 July

Potocki Regiment in 1776 based on Raspe on a Staff officer and an NCO

A private and Lieutenant of the Potocki Regiment, 1791 - 94.

The 7th and 10th Regiments in 1794. MS

8th Foot Regiment Field Hetman of the Crown

The regiment was in existence from 1717 – 1793. It was unique in that its Colonel-in Chief was always the Field Hetman of the Crown Armies. The regiment officially ceased to exist on 2 May 1793 with the surrender of Kamieniec-Podolski during the second partition of Poland. It passed into the service of Russia as the Kamienets Musketeer Regiment. The regiment was originally numbered as three in seniority, then five and finally number eight. From 12.X.1726 the regiment became the Crown Grand Hetman's Regiment. From 1789 the regiment was known as the 8th foot.

Garrisoned: Kamieniec Podolski

Chiefs: Crown Grand Hetmans Stanisław Rzewuski 30.IV.1706 do 12.X.1726; Stanisław Chomętowski 11.X.1726, died 2.IX.1728;Jan Jerzy Ożarowski, around kor. 1728 – 1733, Józef Potocki, Gov. Kiev 1733 – 1746, Jan Klemens Branicki, 1746 – 5 June 1752, Wacław Rzewuski, hetm. 1752 to 9 Apr 1773, Branicki Franc. Ksawery 1773 to 8 Feb 1774; Seweryn Rzewuski 16 Feb 1774 until 1792; Tadeusz Kościuszko 6 Aug 1792

Colonels: Gen. Ripp 1717; Maj Gen Kamphausen (1737), Maj Gen Kamiński (1750); Prince Antoni Lubomirski, Swordbearer. Kor; Maj Gen Każmierski, 1752, Lt. Gen. 1755 – 1761, Michał Kuczyński 13 June 1761, Maj Gen. 20 Nov 1762 until his death on 6 Mar 1778; Marcin Hanicki 1778

The Field Hetman's Regiment in 1756. (Left) an officer in summer dress, (center) officer in winter dress, (right) officer in a winter coat.

The Field Hetman's Regiment in 1775, a staff officer, grenadier officer and an enlisted man.

An officer in the Field Hetman's Regiment, 1791 - 94

Raczynski Regimental officers in 1789. BG

Raczynski Regiment enlisted man 1791 - 94

9th Foot Regiment Raczyński

The regiment was formed in 1776 as the Raczyński Foundation Dragon Regiment by Filip Nereusz Raczyński. In 1789 it was reformed as the 9th Infantry Regiment of the Crown. For a time in 1790 the unit was designated as the tenth regiment, but by 1792 it was returned to the ninth regiment.

Garrisoned: Łowicz 1777 – 1792, part in Wielkopolska, Warsaw 1792, Poznań 1792.

Chief: Filip Raczyński, starosta Mieścicki, Maj Gen. 2 Mar 1768.

Colonels: Ludwig Ferdynand de Tiedemann; Marcin Gisler (1789, 1790), Karol Gordon 28 Sept 1791 – (4.V.) 1793, severely wounded 27 Aug 1794.

Battles and Skirmishes: 1792 Zieleńce 17.VI, Włodzimierz 7 July; **1794** Szczekociny 6 June, Chełm 8 June, Gołków 9 July, Raszyn 10 July, Wola 27 July, Górce 14 Aug, Marymont 26 Aug, Wawrzyszew 27 Aug, Wola 26 Aug, Bielany 1 Sept.

One battalion of the regiment fought at the Battle of Racławice.

Rydzynski Regiment 1775 - 1789. Regimental commander and enlisted man.

Rydzynski Regiment 1791 - 1794. (Left to right) Officer in parade dress, officer in field dress, muskeer

10ᵗʰ *Foot Regiment of the Rydzyński Ordination*

In 1775 the Wojewoda of Kalisz August Sułkowski formed the regiment from soldiers in his private militia. The unit received its army patent from the King on 27 November 1776. In 1789 they were moved to number eleven and in 1794 it was moved to number ten. The last Colonel-in-Chief of the regiment was Ignacy Działyński which caused the regiment to be known later at the Tenth Regiment Działyński.

Garrisoned: Lubar, Kamieniec 1776 - 1793

Chiefs: Prince Jerzy Marcin Lubormirski, Lt. Gen.; Józef de Witte, Maj. Of the Crown Artillery 19 Apr 1779; August Iliński 17.IV.1788, Ignacy Działyński, 1794

Colonels: Maj. Gen Franciszek Pouppart until 1790, Maksymiljan Sierakowski 1790

Battles and Skirmishes: 1792 Boruszkowce 15 June, Zieleńce 17 June, **1794** Warsaw Uprising, Maciejowice

The sharpshooters wore a green uniform with yellow facings. They wore a round cap with a green plume and white leatherwork.

(Left - left to right) Soldier from 1794, Rifleman - black hat, green plume, green uniform with yellow facings, yellow buttons, rifleman - same as previous. Soldier with a navy blue cap, uniform with yellow facings.

Below right - 10th Regiments in 1794. MS

Below left - detail from Norblin's hanging of the traitors showing what appears to be the 10th regiment.

Next page

(Left) The Grenadier Regiment formed in 1775. A private, a non-commissioned officer (note the plume is red over white) and a staff officer.

(Right) The Grenadier Regiment in 1793. An officer and a private

11ᵗʰ Foot Regiment of Grenadiers

This regiment was formed in 1775 by Prince Jerzy Marcin Lubomirski from soldiers of his private militia. In 1776 the regiment was reduced to two battalions, one stationed in Kamieniec and the other in Lubar. The Kamieniec battalion remained the Grenadier Regiment, while the Lubar battalion remained in Lubomorski's army. In 1779 the regiment came under the command of artillery major – Janusz Iliński.

It received line designation number 11 in 1789.From 1788 – 1789 it was re-numbered as the tenth regiment. For a short time in 1790 it was renumbered as the twelfth regiment. By April of that year, it finally settled in as the eleventh regiment.

Garrisoned: Rydzyna, Warszawa 1789, Gniezno 1790, Warsaw 1792.

Chiefs: Prince August Sułkowski, Gov of Kalisz 1 Aug 1775; Maj. Gen. Aleksander Mycielski, 28 Jan 1786; Ignacy Działyński 23 July 1788.

Colonels: R. de Hosson R., Karol de Falckenhayn 1789, Belcour 1789, Maj. Gen. Filip Hauman, Józef Seydlitz until 8 June 1794.

Battles and Skirmishes: **1792** Swisłocz, Zelwa 4 July, Izabelin 5 July, Piaski, Granne 24 July, Krzemień 24 July; **1794** Warsaw Uprising, 17, 18 July, Biał, Nowe – Miasto 3 May, Chełm 8 June, Kurów, Gołków 9 July, Around Warsaw, Wola 27 July and 28 Aug, Maciejowice 10 Oct.

After the Polish- Russo War of 1792, it was transferred into the Russian army in May 1793 as the Mohylewski Regiment of Musketeers.

12ᵗʰ *Foot Regiment of the Crown*

This regiment was first formed in 1775 by Kalikst Poniński but was not admitted to the army rolls until 1778. The unit was designated number twelve, but for a short time in 1790 was renumbered as thirteen.

In May 1793 the regiment was transferred to Russian service as the Izjasławski (Izialav) Grenadier Regiment. According to Nafziger this was part of a group of former Polish regiments that were disbanded in Cudnow 1794 because of the Kościuszko Insurrection.

Garrisoned: Koźmin, Kamieniec 1778, Łabuń 1785, Tulczyn 1789.

Chiefs: Prince Kalist Poniński 19 May 1775, Piotr Alkantara Ożarowski, Castellan of Wojnicki 18 Mar 1785, Prince Józef Lubomirski 17 Mar 1786; Jan Malczewski18 Feb 1788.

Colonels: Aleks Mycielski., Józef Jankowski 1786, Fabjan Ojrzyński 1787, Józef Piotrowski 1792

Battles and Skirmishes: 1792 Boruszkowce 15 June, Zasław, Zielence 17 June, Włodzimierz 7 July, Dubienka 18 July.

Poninski Regiment in 1775. (Left to right) A Staff officer, a private and a private as described on Raspe with the lapels buttoned over. BG

The 12th Regiment 1791 - 1793 in summer dress

129

13th Foot Regiment of the Ostrogski Ordination

This regiment dates back to 1609 under Prince Janusz Ostrogski. After 1776 it was brought into the army rolls and given number designation of thirteen. It kept this for its life except for a short time in 1790 when it was fourteen.

Garrisoned: Dubno

Chiefs: Lt. Gen. Kazimierz Granowski, Governor of Rawski 1766, Inspector of the Crown Army Infantry until 1774; Lipski 1774; Adam Poniński, podskarbi kor. 1776 – 1779; Prince Michaeł Lubormirski 5.IV.1780 – 1794.

Colonels: Michał Mokronowski (1758), Prince Seweryn Lubomirski until 1777; Prince Michał Lubormirski 1777 – 1779; Roch Bogatko May 1780 until 29 May 1782; Ludwig Trokin 29 May 1782; Tomasz Buszyński 2 Aug 1792; Maj. Gen. Stefan Granowski Stefan 1794.

Battles and Skirmishes: 1792 Boruszkowce 15 June, Zieleńce 17 June, Bereżce 18 July, Dubienka 18 July; **1794** Szczekociny 6 June, around Warsaw, Witkowice 13 Aug, Rakowiec 17/18 Aug, Wawrzyszew 27 Aug, Powązki 28 Aug.

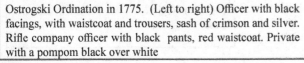

Ostrogski Ordination in 1775. (Left to right) Officer with black facings, with waistcoat and trousers, sash of crimson and silver. Rifle company officer with black pants, red waistcoat. Private with a pompom black over white

(Left) An officer in the Ostrogski Regiment in 1791 - 94. (Right) An private in the 14th Regiment (next page) from the same period.

14th Foot Regiment Potocki

The regiment was first established in 1785 by Szczęsny Potocki from peasants on his estate using equipment from his private army. The regiment was incorporated into the Crown forces in 1786 in Tulczyn as regiment number fourteen. For a short time in 1790 it was renumbered as the seventh regiment.

The regiment participated in the 1792 war against Russia. When Russia tried to incorporate the regiment into its forces following the second partition, the soldiers deserted to Turkey.

Garrisoned: Tulczyn.

Chiefs: Stanisław Szczęsny Potocki, Governor of Ruski, General of the Crown Artillery, until1789; Stanisław Potocki 5 May 1789, Poseł of Lublin;Teodor Potocki 5 Feb 1790

Colonels: Adam Moszczeński; Jakób Lanckoroński 5 Mar 1792, a Maj. Gen. 12 Mar 1794

Battles and Skirmishes: 1792 Boruszkowce 15 June, Zieleńce 17 June, Bereżce 18 July.

15th Foot Regiment of the Crown

The regiment was formed by the Great Sejm in 1792 in response to the coming war with Russia. The regiment was disbanded and reformed between the 1792 war and the Kościuszko Insurrection. The cadre was formed from soldiers of the Guard Infantry Regiment and included a sharpshooter unit.

Garrisoned: Warsaw

Colonels: Jan August Cichocki 4 Mar 1792, Maj Gen. 27 May 1792, Chief 17 Sept 1792

Battles and Skirmishes: **1794** Ostrołęka, Zegrze 18 Aug, Krupczyce 16 Sept, Brześć 17 Oct, Maciejowice 10 Oct, Praga 4 Nov.

In 1794 the riflemen wore a black round hat with a green plume. They wore a green uniform with red distinctions. The leatherwork was black.

16th Foot Regiment of the Treasury

The regiment was formed in 1794 from militia of the Treasury. which was a Pontonier battalion

Garrisoned: Warsaw

Commander: Col. Jan Gisiler

Battles and Skirmishes: 1794 Zegrze 18 Aug, Maciejowice 10 Oct, Praga 4 Nov.

17th Foot Regiment of the Crown

The regiment was formed in April 1794 from volunteers from the Masovia region.

Garrisoned: Warsaw

Commanders: Col Rottenburg; Col. Gregorz Komarnicki

18th Foot Regiment of the Crown

This regiment was formed in April 1794 in part from soldiers discharged from the 5th fusiliers at the expense of Izydor Krasiński, lieutenant of the 5th Fusilier Regiment and the brothers Ossoliński, Castellan of Podlase and Governor of Drohicki, and the Wowode of Tarnowski Podlase. One battalion served in the Nadnarwiańska Division.

Commanders: Col. Izydor Krasiński, Lt. Col. Szuszkowski.

Battles and Skirmishes: **1794** 3,4,5 Apr, Chełm 8 June, before Wąsosz 27 June, Stawiska 3 July, Okrzeja, Słonim 6 Aug, Krupczyce 16 Oct, Brześć 17 Nov, Maciejowice 10 Oct, Praga 4 Nov.

The unit fought at Chełm, Stawiski, Krupczyce, Terespol, Brześć and Maciejowice.

19th Foot Regiment of Crown Riflemen

The regiment was formed in April 1794 by Michał Sokolnicki, the Commander of Wielkopolska.

Formed in April 1794 by Michał Sokolnicki from the people of Wielkopolska Province, it received number 19 in July.

Garrisoned: Warsaw

Commanders: Col. Michał Sokolnicki; Lt. Col. Rymkiweicz, Later Maj. Gen. about 28.VII.

Battles and Skirmishes: 1794 from 20 June and afterward with Gen. Sierkowski, around Warsaw, Marymont 24 July, Krupczyce 16 Sept, Brześć 17 Oct.

(This page left to right) A rifleman of the 19th Regiment. A black giwer with a white over black plume. A white uniform with green turnbacks and pant stripe A rifleman of the 15th Regiment - a black hat with a green plume, red lace, black leatherwork and tan boots. The 20th Regiment private wearing a black uniform with crimson distinctions as well as cap lace. Collar lace was yellow.

(Next page left) The Grenadier Battalion of Krakow based on a series of pictures by Michael Stachowicz, "The Polish Army Camp in 1794". The officer is is the Polisn Army dress, while the peasants are dressed in local dress.

(Next page right) Peasant scythe bearers by Stachowicz.

20th Foot Regiment of the Crown

Formed in June 1794 in Warsaw under the tailor Jan Kiliński

Commander: Col. Jan Kiliński

21st Foot Regiment of the Crown

This regiment was formed in May 1794 in Podlasie by Karwowski and Gen Ziemiański from the estates near Bielski as the Podlaski Pikeman Regiment. It fought against the Prussians at Kolno, Ślosarze and Ostrołęka. In September 1794 it was numbered as regiment twenty-one.

Commander: Col. Leonard Paszkowski

1st Regiment of the Krakow Grenadiers

This regiment was formed after the battle of Racławice in 1794 from the peasant pikeman of the Krakow region. They were armed with scythes, pikes and three hundred muskets. They wore the square topped cap, blue kurtka and a white overcoat. Because of their valor they were nicknamed, "Grenadiers".

The commander wore a black round felt hat with a green plume. His sukmana was white with red collar and cuffs. The embroidery was black. The epaulette on the right shoulder and the lace on the collar were silver. Around his waist he wore a red sash. He had navy pants with a crimson stripe. The shoulder belt was black with a gold plate.

2nd *Regiment of the Krakow Grenadiers*

See above.

Regiment of Lublin Grenadiers

The regiment was formed in May 1794 from peasants of the Lublin region.

Regiment of Sandomierz Grenadiers

Like the Krakow and Lublin Grenadiers, the regiment was formed from peasants in the Sandomierz region in April 1794.

The Janissary Company of the Grand Hetman

The company existed from 1717 – 1775 under the command of the Grand Hetman. They fought against the Bar Confederation (1768 – 1772)

Garrisoned: Near the Crown Grand Hetman

Chief: Crown Grand Hetman 1717 – 1775.

Rotmistrz: Orchowski (1754), Płubiński (1760) – 1775.

Battles and Skirmishes: Confederation of the Bar

1770 – 1789 the hat was a tall red felt hat surrounded by a brass headgear. A white prophet's sleeve hung from the back. The outer jacket was red with black trim along the edges with red pantaloons. Under the jacket they wore a long white caftan with the edges tucked into the belt. The caftan was also edged in black. Boots were black and belts were black studded with brass.

Officers wore brown boots with red pantaloons. They had red kantankas with gold lace and epaulettes and black edging. Under this is a white zupan edged black with gold lace. They wore a red fez with a white turban and white plume.

1710

Private and officer in 1775 by Raspe

(Next page Left) The Grand Hetman and Field Hetman Hungarian Companies, officer (left), privates (right) in 1775 based on Raspe. Note the officers in yellow boots and enlisted in black boots. BG. (Next page right) Field Hetman's Hungarian Company by Raspe, 1775.

Hungarian Company of the Grand Hetman of the Crown

The company existed from 1717 to 1789, then again in 1793. They were stationed wherever the Grand Hetman had his headquarters.

Chief: Crown Grand Hetman 717 - 1789

Rotmistrz: Col. Karski (1754);Stanisław Bartochowski 1760, Col. As of 1761; Jakób Załęski (1775); removed 20 Aug 1778; Antoni Gozdowski

Garrisoned: Near the person of the Crown Grand Hetman.

Crown Hungarian Company 1764 wore a braided light blue dolman with gold lace and yellow cuffs – red for officers. Light blue pants, officers with gold Hungarian knots on the thighs. There is a red sash. The enlisted men wore a black mirliton, for officers this had a wing and white feathers in the front. They are pictured with red delias.

1775 – 1789. A white Attila was worn underneath. For officers the braid and edging was gold, for troopers, it was red. Officers wore a mirliton with sleeve edged in gold and a white plume and cockade. Troopers wore a kuczma style hat with black fur, black plume and a hanging red bag. All ranks wore white Hungarian britches with red and gold Hungarian knots. Around their waist they had a red barrel belt. Officers wore yellow boots and ranks wore black. All ranks wore a red sabretache with a white Polish eagle in the center. The officer's was edged in gold, ranks in green.

Hungarian Company of the Field Hetman of the Crown

The company existed from 1717 to 1789, then again in 1793. They were stationed wherever the Field Hetman had his headquarters.

Chief: The Crown Field Hetman 1717-1789
Rotmistrz: Bułła (1754 – 1764); Piotr Tyszkiewicz (1775), dismissed 16.XII.1783; Jakób Tyszkiewicz; Colonel Paprocki (1789); Jakób Tyszkiewicz 1793
This unit wore the same uniform as above but reversed the red and green.

Hungarian Company of the Great Marshal of the Crown

The company existed from 1717 to 1789, then again in 1793. They were stationed wherever the Great Marshall had his headquarters.

The Hungarian Company of the Provost Marshall's was nicknamed "The Blackbirds"

Chief: The High Crown Marshall, 1717 – 1794
Commander: Rotm. Jan Fournier (1754 – 1787); Piotr Hoffman (1793)
Battles and Skirmishes: The Warsaw Uprising, 17 and 18 Apr 1794, Area around Warsaw.

Garrison of Krakow
1794. They are pictured by Stachowicz wearing the regulation casquet, but with the white crest side to side.

(Left) The Grand Marshal of the Crown's Hungarian Company. They were called the "Blackbirds" and acted as policemen. The caps were blue with yellow metal. in 1775. The third figure is a militia man from Krakow in 1787. He is wearng a brass cap, dark blue jacket with crimson turnbacks and yellow buttons.

(Right) The Grand Marshal's company by Raspe in 1775.

(Left) Artilleryman from the Krakow garrison in 1794 by Michal Stachowicz.

(Right) NCO of the riflemen regiment for the garrison of Krakow 1794. The crest in this case is traverse instead of fore and aft.

(Bottom right) The militia from Warsaw in the early 18th century. (left) A white cap, dark blue coat, collar and cuffs magenta, yellow shoes. (Middle and right) Warsaw milita from the 1720's. Black hats with white lace. Green coat with scarlet facings. White vests with gold braid, scarlet trousers, black stockings, white leatherwork and gold braid.

(Below left) Artillery and infantry of the Krakow garrison by Stachowicz

Warsaw Militia

The Warsaw Militia of the 1760's was dressed in light blue jackets and pants. They had either a zupan or vest underneath in yellow/buff – the same as the turnbacks. The hat was either a tricorne or fur colpak in black.

1794 – The local militias were dress part civilian and part military. The prevalent headgear seems to have been a stovepipe hat, liberty cap or square topped hat.

(Left) Militia of Warsaw 1750 - 1763 by Bruhl

(Right) Militia of Warsaw 1749

Urban militia of Warsaw in 1794. (Left to right) Black hat with white over red plume. Blue jacket with crimson lapels, white waistcoat and trousers. This is from the Norblin painting on the Hangings (See next page). Next a militia officer in black hat, blue jacket, light blue colar and cuffs. A citizen in the uniform of the municipal guard - blue jacket, crimson distinctions, white pants. Militia officer - hat of lambs wool, blue jacket and trousers with crimson distinctions.

Friekorps of 1792

Freikorps were units raised by individuals or local government on an ad-hoc basis

1st Battalion of Light Infantry Volunteers
Formed by de Süssmilch, 22 May 1792, disbanded in October after Targowica.
Commander: Jan Gottfried de Süssmilch of the 6th Łancowy 26 May 1792

2nd Battalion of Light Infantry Volunteers
Formed by Rottenburg, 22 May 1792, disbanded in October after Targowica.
Commander: Lt. Col. Rottenburg ppłk. 16. May 1792, in 1794 commanders of the 17th Infantry regiment

3dr Battalion of Light Infantry Volunteers – Grand Duchy of Lithuania
Formed by Captain Trębicki, 22 May 1792, dissolved after Targowica on 23 September 1792
Commander: Lt. Col. Michał Trębicki 28 May 1792

4th Battalion of Light Infantry Volunteers
Formed 15 June 1792 by Niedermeier, an officer of the Bar Confederation, dissolved in October after Targowica
Commander: Niedermeier

(Left) The detail of a militia officer from Norblin. (Center) Volunteers from 1794 - left figurea black giwer, navy blue uniform with yellow distinctions. A grey coat with natural lining based on a sketch by Norblin which is shown on the next panel. Center figure is a Masowian commander in blue jacket, crimson distinctions, white piping, yellow epaulets and white trousers. (Right) Volunteer cavalry in dark blue with green distinctiond, yellow button. Knotel has the colors as crimsonfor the peliesse, collar and trousers with a green dolman. BG

Volunteers of 1794

Many of the units raised in 1794 were volunteers organized into small operational units. They wore either a black kiwer with a white plume or broad brimmed hat, some with the left side pinned up. One sketch by Norblin shows a grey three-quarters lengthen overcoat lined white.

Crown Lands Militia

These units were originally formed from peasants from the Crown lands. They consisted of infantry units from Ukrainian, Ruskie and Wielkopolska.

The pontonier battalion was originally formed from the Crown Militia.

Crown Treasury (Skarbowa) Militia

Formed in 1763 as the Crown Treasury Grenadier Company; 1777 it was known as the Crown Treasury Militia Corps; Pontonier Battalion; from 17 IX 1789 The Treasury Battalion; from 1794 it was the 16[th]Regiment of Infantry

Commander: Capt. Skwarczyński (1763); Col. Markowski (1777); Col. De Woyten, died 1788; Col. Jan Gisiler.

Battles: Warsaw Uprising 17 Apr 1794.

The Garrison of Częstochowa

Commander: Maj. Marcin Wierzbowski (1787).

UNITS FROM CROWN LANDS IN 1794

Maj Gen Baranowski's Command

Maj. Biegański's Rifles
Battles and Skirmishes: Szczęśiliwice 17/18 Aug, Praga 4 Nov.

Czyż's Rifle Battalion.

Czyżewski's Command
Battles and Skirmishes: Raszowa and Mohyla 27 June

Capt. Dembiński's Rifles
Battles and Skirmishes: Szczęśliwice 29 July.

Col Florjan Dembowski's Rifle Battalion
Battles and Skirmishes: Maciejowice 10 Oct, Praga 4 Nov

Cap. Ludwik Dembowski's Rifles
Battles and Skirmishes: Wola 30 July, around Warsaw 8/9 Aug.

Lt. Col. Hemling's Battalion

Januszkiewicz's Rifles
Battles and Skirmishes: Nieporęt 25 Aug

Krakow Grenadier Battalion (Scythmen)
Formed 4 Apr,
Commanders: Jan Ślaski Jan; Taszycki; Maj Gen. Ziemiański Wojewoda of Krakow, Col. Krzycki, Lt. Col. Siemianowski;Col. Kropiński, Col. Jabłonowski.
Battles and Skirmishes: Racławice 4 Apr, Szczekociny 6 July, around Warsaw, Wola 27 Aug, Rakowiec 17/18 Aug, Maciejowice 10 Oct, Praga 4 Nov.

Michałowski's Detachment

Warsaw Municipal Volunteer Battalion
Commanders: Jan Rafałow, Col. Królikowski
Battles and Skirmishes: Słonim 2/3 Aug, Krupczyce 16 Sept, Brześć 17 Sept, Maciejowice 10 Oct, Praga 4 Nov.

Lt. Col. Niewiadomski's detachment

Riflemen of Col. Ossowski
Battles and Skirmishes: Praga 4 Nov.

Col. Piotrowski's Volunteers

Rifle Battalion of Lt. Col. Franciszek Ksawery Rymkiewicz
Battles and Skirmishes: Górce 23 Aug, Wawrzyzsew 28 Aug.

Riflemen of Starzeński
Battles and Skirmishes: Praga 4 Nov.

The Rifle Regiment of Lt. Col. Węgierski

Skalski's Volunteer Regiment

The rebel camp in 1794 by Stachowicz. From the left, soldiers of the 4th Reg. (Grand Hetman's Regiment), 7th Reg., a scytheman, artilleryman, scytheman, soldiers of the 3rd and 13th Reg. In the middle group a scytheman, an officer, Advance Guard, scytheman, artillery officer, a soldier of the 10th Reg., an officer of the 13th Reg. and a rifleman of the 3rd Reg. On the right is a soldier of the 7th Reg and a Scytheman. Behind them is a Pocztowy and officer of the National Cavalry

LEVY OF THE COMMONWEALTH AND CROWN MILITIA FOR 1794

Troops of Bielski
> **Leader**: Gen. Ziemiański;Wilhielm Orsetii Karwowski 1 August
> **Skirmishes:** Kumelsk 1 July, Lachów 1 July, Stawiski 3 July, around Rajgrod 7 July, Nowogród 22 Sept.

Troops of Bloński: Adam Szymanowski; Stanisław Dzimiński

Troops of Brasława: Maj. Gen. Bielikowicz,

The Province of Brzesko-Kujawa: Maj. Gen. Mniewski,

Troops of Chełm: Col. Zagórski,

Troops of Czersa: Gen. Wodzińsk starosta of nurski,

Troops of Drohicki
> **Skirmishes:** Praga 4 Nov.

Troops of Garwolińa: Maj. Gen. Adam Skulski
> **Skirmishes:** around Ryka 23 August

Area of Gnieźno: Maj. Gen. Lipski,

Area of Gostyńa: Kazimierz Dąbrowski

Rifle Battalion of Kalice Battalion: attached to the 5th regiment, Capt.Kowwacz
> **Skirmishes:** around Serocka 29 May.

Militia of Krakow: Maj. Gen.Wieniawski
> **Skirmishes:** around Promnika 14 June (part of the Krakow Grenadier Battalion)

Troops of Livonia: Col. Sokolnicki

Troops of Lublin: Maj. Gen. Piotr Potocki, Starosta of Szczyrzycki,

Militia Regiment of Lublin: Józef Trzciński 15 May, removed 12 Sept, Lt. Col Tyszkiewicz

Lublin Grenadier Battalion: Col. Pągoski

Łęczycka Cavalry: Kryże.

Troops of Łomżyńa: Rifles under Gen. Wiszowata
> **Skirmishes:** around Ostrołęką 19 Aug, Grabowo 25 Aug.

Duchy of Mazowia: Maj. Gen. Stanisław Mokronowski , 19 Apr, Maj. Gen. Orłowski to 17 June.

Troops of Mielnick: Maj Gen. Radzimiński,
>   **Skirmishes:** around Wolą 28 Aug.

Troops of Nurska: Maj. Gen. Zieliński,
>   **Skirmishes**: around Narwią 25 Aug, at Troszczynem 14 Sept

The Province of Podlaise: Maj Gen. Karwowski (Cavalry and Infantry)

The Province of Pomorsze: Maj. Gen. Kruszyński

The Province of Poznań: Maj. Gen. Niemojewski 22 Sept.

Troops of Radom: Col. Dobek, until captured
>   **Skirmishes:** 15 June around Lipow Pola, Gawdzicki

The Province Rawa: Maj. Gen. Woyczyński

The Province of Sandomiersz: Maj. Gen. Józef Służewski 10 Apr. Grenadier Battalion: (Scythemen): Lt. Cols: Ożarowski and Pągowski,
>   **Battle:** fought at Szczekociny 6 June. Militia: Lt. Col. Kirkor

The Lands of Sochaczewski: Maj. Gen. Lipski 23 Aug, Maj. Gen. Bielicki 30 Sept.

The Province of Sieradzki: Maj. Gen. Zbijewski 23 Aug.

Troops of Stężycki: Maj.Gen. Radzymiński. Cavalry Regiment "Golden Freedom" Maj Gen. Zgliczyński, Infantry battalion: Ignacy Boski

The Area of Tarczyński: Fabjan Kleszczyński

Troops of Warsaw: Maj. Gen. Stanisław Szymanowski Stan., Maj. Gen. Młocki

The County of Warsaw: Jakób Młocki, Józef Woyna, Sokołowski, Jan Skwarski

The Province of Wielkopolska: (Scythemen), the capture of Bydgoszczy 2 Oct.

Troops of Wieluńka (The Uprising): Maj. Gen Leonardwicz,

Troops of Wizka (Rifles and cavalry) Maj Gen Chryzantem Opacki 27 June, Col. Rajmund Rembieliński 27 June.

Crown Cavalry in the 18th Century

Guard Cavalry of the Crown

The Guard cavalry was a dragoon regiment also known as the *Mirowska Dragoons*. They also included a contingent of Cossacks as part of the regiment. In addition to the dragoons, there were at different times, hussar and pancerni squadrons attached to the King.

Guard Crown Cavalry Regiment *(Cron leib Garde Dragoner)*

Garrisoned: Warsaw, Kraków
Chiefs: Fieldmarshal Jakób Henry Fleming. (1717), Prince Stanisław Lubomirski. Lt. Gen, Starosta of Bohusław, Senshal (cześnik) of the Crown (1754) – 1760, Kazimirz Poniatowski,Lt. Gen.;Crown Chamberlain;Brother of the King (1760);Wincenty Potocki 6 Dec 1773, Crown Chamberlain until 1793; Prince Stanisław Poniatowski 1794.
Colonels: Wilhielm Mier (1717); Karol Jordon, Maj.Gen. (1767), Henry Lettow Mar 1774, Józef Hofman (1787) Dyonizy Poniatowski, Maj. Gen. 23.V.1794
Battles and Skirmishes: The Bar Confederation, The Warsaw Uprising 17 Apr 1794, Słonim 3 Aug. Krupczyce 16 Sept, Brześć 17 Sept, Maciejowice 10 Oct.

1760 – 1789 The Crown Guard Dragoons were dressed like their Saxon forbearers in buff coats and breeches, tricorne hat. They had red turnbacks and white (silver) lace. For full dress occasions they wore a red, edged talbard to simulate a cuirass. Black high topped boots. The saddle cloth was crimson with silver edges and eagle in the back corner. The standard was a crimson banner with a silver Polish eagle and edging.

1790 – 1795 The Crown Guard Dragoon adopted red jackets with blue facings and yellow buttons. A leather peaked cap with crest and visor typical of light cavalry of the period. Some had leopard skin around the base and horsehair mane.

1794 - Dragoon Guards Artillery had a black round felt helmet with a visor and brass band. They had a green kurtka and trousers with yellow buttons. The unit color was with red for cuffs, facings and side stripe. Leather belting is white.

Bacciarelli shows Prince Poniatowski in uniform as commander of the Guards in a buff coat and pants with blue distinctions, a light dragoon crested helmet and a breastplate. The saddle cloth was crimson with three rows of gold lace. The royal cipher and crown were angled in the corner in silver

They took part in fighting from the Bar Confederation through the Warsaw Insurrection. As such they fought in the battles at Słonim, Krupczyce, Brześć, and Maciejowice.

Crown Dragoon Guard Cavalry from the time of Augustus II. Black hats with white or silver lace. Crimson jackets. BG

Officers in service and parade dress in 1732 based on Mock's painting of the Polish encampment

In 1775 in ordinary dress, crimson coat with blue distinctions.white waistcoat and trousers. Silver braid. Brass bindings

1775 by Raspe of Officer and trooper

Parade uniform cap of the Guard Cavalry, 1791. PAM

(Left to right) Horse Guards in a gray coat with black hat with white lace and plume and brass fittings. Gunner in 1794, black cap with brass binding green jacket, crimson distinctions and yellow buttons. Dragoon in service dress 1794, red jacket with blue distinctions.

1st Brigade of National Cavalry (1st Wielkopolski)

The brigade was formed in 1776 from hussar and pancerni banners from Wielkopolska. At the end of 1789 the banners of the brigade were numbered from 1 to 24 in the 1st National Cavalry.

Garrisoned: Szreńsk, Rypin, Raciąż, Sulmierzyce, Stawiszyn, Pyzdry, Gniezno (1792), Ryczywół, Koło, Pułtusk (1794) Ostrołęka.

Commanders: Maj. Gen. Stanisław Łuba, Starosta Stawiszyńska, from 9 Dec 1783 until his death; Damazy Mioduski, from 26 June 1790 until 9 July. 1792; Antoni Madaliński, from 14 July 1792.

Battles and Skirmishes: 1792 - Szreńsk, Wyszogród, Łowicz, Stara Rawa. **1794** - Inowłódź 21 Mar, Końskie 1 Apr, Racławice 4 Apr, Szczekociny 6 June, Końskie 26 June, Starczyska 29 June, Environs of Warsaw, Gołków 9 July, Czerniaków 31 July, Lachy 19 Aug.

2nd Wielkopolska Brigade in 1776. An officer, Towarzysz and Pocztowy. GB

1st Wielkopolska Brigade in 1775 according to Raspe. A Towarszysz and Pocztowy

1st Wielkopolska Brigade in 1790. A captain Towarzysz in cloak, Towarzysz and Pocztowy. BG

1st Wielkopolska Brigade wearing cape in 1790. Artist Unknown

Pocztowy 1st Wielkopolska Brigade in 1790. Artist Unknown

Trumpeter of the 1st Brigade in 1794 by Michal Stachowicz

2nd *Brigade of National Cavalry (2nd Wielkopolski)*

This unit was formed 30.XI.1789 from units of the 1st Wielkopolska Brigade.

Garrisoned: Warta, Kozienice (1792), Kościan, skirmish at the Obrą and Wartą, Przedbórz (1793), Chęciny, Włodzimierz (Nov. 1794), Kowel.
Commanders: Paweł Biernacki, Castellan of Sieradzki, 14.X.1789
Battles and Skirmishes: **1792** - Zieleńce 17 June, Dubniki 8 July, Dubienka 18 July. **1794** - Racławice 4 Apr, Szczekociny 6 June, Environs of Warsaw, Zbarz, Rakowice 17/18 Aug.

3rd *Brigade of National Cavalry (1st Małopolska)*

This unit was formed 30 Nov1789 from units of the 1st Wielkopolska and 3rd Ukraińian.

Garrisoned: Małopolska, Wiślica, Stobnica, Nowe Miasto and thereabout. (1790), Sandomierz (Mar 1792), Bielsk (Oct 1792) and from Brańska to Łomża.
Commanders: Józef Golejowski, until his death;Piotr Hadziewicz 20 Feb 1790, promoted to Maj. Gen. 18 Oct 1793;Kajetan Ożarowski (son of the hetman), until 8 June 1794; Józef Rzewuski.
Battles and Skirmishes: **1792** - Zieleńce 17 June. **1794** - Stanisławów 26 Apr, Chełm 8 June, Uściług 28 June, Environs of Warsaw, Gołchów 29 June, Witkowice 13 Aug, Strzyże 24 Sept, Maciejowice 10 Oct.

4th *Brigade of National Cavalry (2nd Małopolska)*

This unit was formed 30 XI 1789

Garrisoned: Krasnystaw to Augustowa (1790), 8 banners were at Wołyniu (Połonne), 4 in Mazowiecka (Mar 1792) 2 squadrons at Warszaw, the rest were at Solcu and the vicinity (Oct 1793).
Commanders: Jan Eryk Potocki; Adam Walewskin 1793. (Vicebrigadier Commander 1794); Ludwik Manget; Jażwiński.
Battles and Skirmishes: 1792 - Granne 24 July 1794 - Kozubowo 25 Mar, Opatów 29 Mar, Racławice 4 Apr, Szczekociny 6 June, around Warszawy, Sielec 17 Sept, Rzewnie 18 Sept, Kadniewek, Gzowo, Strzyże 20 and 24 Sept.

 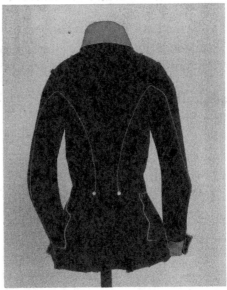

National Cavalry Kurtka from the period 1789 - 1794. PAM

Cap of the Towarszysz in the nation cavalry brigaed 1789 - 1794. PAM

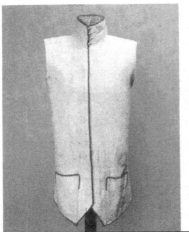

National Cavalry waistcoat for the years 1789 - 1794. PAM

5th Brigade of National Cavalry (3rd Ukrainian)

This unit was formed in 1776 from banners of hussars and pancerni from the Ukraine and Podolska as the 3rd Ukrainian Brigade. At the end of 1789 they received banner numbers 49 to 72, they were incorporated into the Russian Army as Dnieprski Brigade 6.V.1793.

Garrisoned: Half -brigade – Białocerkiew, Mohylów, Targowica, 8 banners at Małopolska (1779 – 1792)

Commanders: Stefan Lubowidzki , 1 Sept.1776, a Maj. Gen in 12.XII.1783;Jan Świejkowski, 24.VII (1 Aug) 1792.

Battles and Skirmishes: 1792 - Motowiłówka 11 June, Boruszkowce 15 June, Zieleńce 17 June, Dubienka 18 July.

(Left) Captains of the Pancerni Squadrons 1764 - 1775.

(Right) The 3rd Ukrainian of the National Cavalry Brigades in 1775. An officer, Towarszysz and Pocztowi formed from Hussars and Pancerni squadrons from Ukrain and Podolia

(Left) Brigadiers of the 3rd Ukrainian. In 1792 crimson hat, facings, and stripes on saddle cloth. Silver trim. A Brigadier in 1789, navy kontusz with crimson lining, white zupan, yellow boots and silver sash

3rd Ukrainian in 1792, navy blue kurtka and pants, scarlet turnbacks and silver braid. Black felt hat with white lace. A Brigadier in 1789, same colors but with scarlet trousers and silver braid.

6th Brigade of National Cavalry (2rd Ukraińian)

6th Brigade of National Cavalry (2rd Ukraińian)

This unit was formed in 1776 from hussar and pancerni banners that at the end of 1789 received the squadron numbers 73 to 96 as the 4th Brigade. They were incorporated into the Russian Army as the Dniestrzański Regiment, 6.V.1793.

Garrisoned: Ukraińe, Białocerkiew, Łabuń (1779), Mohylów, Żwaniec and thereabouts, Tulczyn (1789), Jampol (1792), Janowiec on the Wisłą (IX.1792), on the Dniepr in 1793.

Commanders: Michał Zielonka, 1.IX.1776, made a Maj. Gen. 11.XII. 1783, until his death; Roch Jerlicz 28.V.1786 Maj. Gen.; Maciej Perekładowski Maj. Gen. 1793

Battles and Skirmishes: **1792** - Serby 22 May, Nowa Sieniawka 11 June, Zieleńce 17 June, Berezie 18 July, Markuszów 26 July.

2nd Ukrainina in 1776 according to Raspe. An officer, Towarzysz and Pocztowy

2nd Ukrainian by Gabriel Raspe

7th Brigade of National Cavalry (1st Ukraińian)

The Brigade was formed in 1776 from hussar and pancerni banners from the Ukraine and Podolska. In 1789 the banners received designation 25-48 in the National Cavalry strength, or Brigade number 3. They were incorporated into the Russian Army as the Bracławski Regiment on 6.VI.1793.

Garrisoned: Ukraine and Podola, Szarogród until 1792, Zwinogród and the vicinity (during the 1792 War).

Commanders: Rafał Dzierżek 1.IX. 1776, as Maj. Gen. 10.XII. 1783; Stanisław Kublicki 27.VI. 1793; Franciszek Ksawary Wyszkowski.

Battles and Skirmishes: **1792** - Dubienka 18 May, Serby and Cerkinówka 22 May, Mórafa 26 May, Zieleńce 17 June. **1794** - Białorękawy 30 April, Stary Konstantynów 1 May, Chełm 8 June, Włodzimierz 7 July, Bereże 18 July, Around Warszaw, Gołchów 9 July, Raszyn 10 July, Wola 27 July, Powązki 18 August, Wawrzyszew 28 August.

1st Ukrainian from 1776 to 1789, made up of Hussars and Pancerni squadrons. An officer, Towarzysz and Pocztowy

1st Ukrainian by Raspe

8th Brigade of National Cavalry (4th Ukrainian)

The brigade was formed in 1789 and in 1793 was to be transferred to Russian service under the name Wołyński Brigade.

Garrisoned: Humań and from Bohopol to Czehryn (1790), Granów (Mar 1792), Jampol and the vicinity (Oct 1792)

Commanders: Wielhorski; Stanisław Mokronowski, a Maj.Gen. in 1 Aug.1792; Prince Eustachy Sanguszko 1 Aug 1792; Franciszek Łażniński, a Brig. Gen. from 23 June 1794;Benedykt Kołyszko 23 June 1794, Brig Gen. as of 17 Sept.

Battles and Skirmishes: **1792** - Motowiłowka 11 June, Zasław, Wiszniopol 14 June, Boruszkowce 15 June, Zieleńce 17 June; **1794** – Vicinity of Warszawy, Sochaczew 1 July, 4 July, Błonie 9 July, Powązki 28 July, Górce 14 Aug, Powązki 18 Aug, Tokary and Witkowice 28 Aug, Żuków and Kamionna 4 Oct, along the Bzurą River 6 Oct.

In Kossak's painting of Eustachy Sanguszko regiment in 1792, they seem to be wearing an older version of the cavalry uniform with red distinctions. They are pictured with blue kontusz with red cuffs. Underneath was a red zupan with blue pants. The headgear was a black colpak with a red bag and white feather cockade. The lance pennant was red over white. Trumpeters had a red jacket with light blue collar, cuffs and turnbacks. They wore light blue pants with a white stripe down the side. He had a black mirliton with white cords. The horse blanket was red with a light blue edging.

4th Ukrainian in 1792 by Julisz Kossak

155

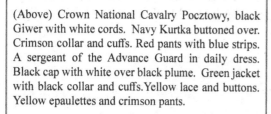

(Above) National cavalry in 1794 - Pocztowy in black giwer, white over black plume, navy jacket with crimson turnbacks, crimson pants, white stripes, iron scabbard. Towarzysz in a white cape-coat, blue lacecrimson collar, blue trousers with scarlet stripes. Towarzysz 1791 in crimson cap, gold cross, navy jacket and torusers with crimson stripe. Iron scabbard

(Above) Crown National Cavalry Pocztowy, black Giwer with white cords. Navy Kurtka buttoned over. Crimson collar and cuffs. Red pants with blue strips. A sergeant of the Advance Guard in daily dress. Black cap with white over black plume. Green jacket with black collar and cuffs.Yellow lace and buttons. Yellow epaulettes and crimson pants.

(Right) Towarzysz of the Wielkopolska Cavalry Brigade 1775 - 1785. Black lambskin white and blue top. Navy blue trousers and jacket, crimson turnbacks and pant stripe, white vest. Officer in off-duty dress in red cap with white plume and black lambskin, white zupan, dark blue kontusz with red facings, silver sashand yellow boots. Mounted officer crimson top with black band and white plume, navy blue jacket and pants with crimson facings and stripe and silver lace.

1st Regiment of the Queen's Advance Guard

This was formed in 1789 from the Dragoon Regiment of Maj. Gen. Szdłowski

Garrisoned: Cudnów, Powołocza, Warszawa (1794).

Chief: Krysztof Karwicki 6 Mar 1789, a Maj. Gen. as of 1 Aug 1792

Colonels: Wielowiejski; Gorzeński

Battles and Skirmishes:1792 - Burakowski's Tavern 11 June, Raczki 12 June, Boruszkowce 15 June, Zieleńce 17 June, Włodzimierz 7 July, Dubienka 18 July. 1794 - Warszawa 17 June, Szczekociny 6 June, the environs of Warszaw, Szczęśliwice, Strzyże 24 Sept, Praga 4 Nov.

(Below)Advance Guard of the Crown. Hat has a crimson top, black band and white plume. Navy blue uniform with crimson distinctions, gold buttons and lace. Towarzysz as above with penant crimson over blue and white. Trumpeter with black giwer, whit lace and plume. Kurtka red with blue facings yellow buttons. Towarzysz in 1790 - 94 kontusz colors as above.

(Above) Towarzysz of the light cavalry. The arrows and quiver are covered with a waterskin to protect it from rain. A lieutantant holds a war hammer in his hand. All three figures are from the painting by Mock.

(Above) 1st Advance Guard Regiment of the Crown made up from nine squadrons of light cavalry in 1789. A Towarzysz, an officer and a Pocztowy based on Raspe.

2nd Regiment of Advance Guard of the Crown

This regiment was formed from the Grand Hetman's Dragoons in 1789. It was incorporated into the Russian Army as the Żytomirski regiment in 6 May 1793.

Garrisoned: Mohilow, Chwastów, Czeczelnik (1792).

Chief: The Grand Hetman of the Crown

Colonel: Józef Zajączek. 1789 do 4.VI.1792.

Battles and Skirmishes: 1792 - Zieleńce 17 June, Włodzimierz 8 July.

1790 – 1794 for troopers the saddle cloth was black with red trim, for towarzysz and officers it was red with a white cloth.

2nd Advance Guard Regiment formed in 1776

Grand Hetman's Advanced Guard Regiment in 1790 based on drawings by Haraisomicz

3rd Regiment of Advance Guard of the Crown

This was formed from the Field Hetman's Dragoons in 1789.

Garrisoned: Łuck, Chmielnik, Kowel (1792)

Chief: The Field Hetman of the Crown; Józef Zajączek in 4.V.1792, as Maj. Gen. from 26.V.1792.

Colonels: Kościelski 1789; Michał Kobyłecki 1790; Michał Zagórski 1794.

Battles and Skirmishes: 1792 - Zieleńce 17 June, Dubienka 18 July. 1794 - Chełm 8 June, Uściług 28 June, around Warszaw, Powązki 28 July and 18 Aug.

1779 – 1789 Saddle cloth was dark blue with red edging.
1794 –The trumpeters wore a red giver, with a white plume tipped red. Trumpeters wore white jackets with blue facings edged gold. Trousers were red with white stripe. Trumpeters wore gold and red shoulder straps edged in gold. The saddle cloth was dark blue, edged gold with a red central stripe. The pistol holder was just edged gold.

3rd Advanced Guard Regiment - Field Hetman in 1794. A Pocztowy, Officer and Trumpter based on a drawing by Alexander Orlowski	4th Advanced Guard Regiment in 1775 by Raspe	5th Advanced Guard Regiment in 1775 by Raspe

4th Regiment of the Crown Advance Guard of Prince Württemberg

Formed in 1776 from light cavalry banners. It was incorporated into the Russian Army under the Konstantynowski Regiment 6 May1793.

Garrisoned: Warta, Czechryń (Oct 1792)

Chief's: Arnold Anastarzy Byszewski, Crown Equery 8 June. 1789, Maj. Gen. and later Lt. Gen. 9 April 1791;

Colonel: Józef Byszewski. 13 Jan 1778

Battles and Skirmishes: 1792 - Izabelin 7 July, Mścibów 10 July. 1794 - Racławice April, Warsaw, Brześć, 17 Sept, Skalmierz, Szczekociny 6 June, Chełm 8 June Krupczyce 16 Sept,.

1772 – 1789 the musicians had gold lace added to the arms and lapels as well as swallow wings on the shoulders. The saddle cloth was green with red stripes and gold eagles.

1794 Trumpeter white jacket, black distinctions, red pants with yellow stripe. Black mirliton with white plume tipped red. Red over sash edged in gold. The saddle cloth blue with white and red stripes separated with gold edging.

5th Regiment of the Crown Advance Guard of Prince Lubomirski

Formed in 1776 from light cavalry banners. It was incorporated into the Russian Army under the Iziasławski (also known as Zasławski) 6 May 1793.

Garrisoned: Tetyów, Berszada (1787), Czeczelnik (1789), Wiśniowiec and the area. (Oct 1792)

Chief: Kajetan Miączyński 11 Nov 1778;Jan Malczewski 22 Feb 1783; Prince Józef Lubomirski 18 Nov 1788.

Colonel: Józef Wiesiołowski;Jan Stępkowski 1 May 1783; Maj. Gen. Ignacy Kamiński

Battles and Skirmishes: 1792 - Wiszniopol 14 June, Boruszkowce 15 June, Zieleńce 17 June. 1794 - Szczekociny 6 June, around Warszawy, Błonie 9 July, Czerniaków 31 July, Krupczyce 16 July, Brześć 17 Sept, around Biała 27 Sept, Maciejowice 10 Oct.

1st Regiment of the Loyal Cossacks of Jan Potocki

This regiment was formed from western Cossacks in May 1792. Its first leader was Jan Potocki, who was a major in the National Cavalry. In October 1792 they became the Kiev Light Cavalry Regiment of the Targowice Confederation.

Leader: Jan Potocki, Rotmitzer of the National Cavalry Kawal. Narodowej, Starosta of Kaniowa, and Master of Poznań.

1792 – This unit wore a black lamb's wool kolpak with a red bag. They wore a black kontusz and pants piped white along the trim and on the pants side stripe. Beneath the kontusz was a red zupan, also piped in white along the pointed cuffs and the turned down collar. The pant stripe had a yellow center stripe. They wore a crimson sash and black boots. The lance had no pennant. A brown camel hair burqa was worn over their shoulders in bad weather

Cossacks based on Norblin. The cossack on the right is wearing a burqa - a longhair woven camel's hair, lightweight cape against the elements

Uniformed in black, the zupan and caps were crimson, white turnbacks and black boots.

2nd Regiment of Loyal Cossacks of Poniatowski/Chomentowski

This regiment was formed in May 1792 by Prince Czartoryski. The first colonel was Józef Poniatowski and in June 1792 Michał Chomentowski. The recruits came from the seches of Berzadski, Korsuński and Granowski. The regiment became part of the Kiev Light Cavalry Regiment of the Targowica Confederation. Eventually it became the Bohski Light Cavalry Regiment in the Russian Army.

Leader: Colonel Józef Poniatowski 4 June1792

Battles and Skirmishes: 1792 - Dubienka 18 July.

The 1ˢᵗ Regiment of the King's Lancers and Commonwealth Light Cavalry (or King's Own Uhlan)

Formed in 1710. This was the first regiment to be designated a Lancer Regiment.

Garrisoned: Warszawa, Łomazy (1774), Korsuń (1787), Kozienice (1794).

Colonel: Wojno; Stanisław Kening (1783); Franciszek Wojciechowski (1794)

Battles and Skirmishes: Bar Confederation 1768 – 1772; 1794 - Warszawa 17 April, Nowy Dwór 26 April, Słonim 3 Aug, Zegrze 18 Aug, Krupczyce 16 Sept, Brześć 17 Sept, Maciejowice 10 Oct, Praga 4 Nov.

The King's Lancers in 1775 by Raspe

Kings lancers - Two Towarzycz in 1768 and an officer. Hats crimson with black lambskin. Plume of the soldiers are crimson and officer white. Green jacket with yellow braid and crimson turnbacks. Vest and trousers crimson. Yellow boots for the officer. Crimson - green penant. Saddle cloth crimson

Pocztowy of the King's Lancers in 1775 and a Towarzycz of the King's Lancer in 1770.

King's Lancer Pocztowy with black giwer, green jacket, with crimson distinctions. Crimson mantel crimson and saddle cloth with green stripe. Crimson trousers with green stripe. Pennant green and crimson. Jozef Poniatowski as the head of the regiment

1st Regiment of the King's Lancers. Pocztowy with green jacket crimson distinctions and pants. Green stripe on the trousers. Saddle cloth is brigth red with green stripe. A towarzycz with the colors as above. Lance 300 cm and penant 50 cm wide. Pennant crimson and green in four parts. Senior officer were a green kontusz and white zupan.

Dragoons of the Crown Army

Kings' Regiment of Horse

This regiment was formed in 1717 and converted to the King's 1st Advance Guard Regiment in 1789.

Garrisoned: Krakow and Sandomiersz Provinces (1717), *Łabuń* 1777, Cudnów 1778

Chief: Lt. Gen. Joachim Fryderyk Flemming, 1717 – 1724; Jan Jerzy Fleming 1724;Maj. Gen. Józef Mniszech Starosta of Sanock, 1726;Maj. Gen. Tadeusz Kozłowski 20 Apr 1774; Adam Szydłowski 25 Sept 1783, Starosta of Mielnica.

Colonels: Maj. Gen. (1772) Adam Wielowiejski 1774 until his death in 1783; Stanisław Wielowiejski 7.V.1783.

Prince's Dragoon Regiment in 1732 based on Mock. The chief of the Regiment and an enlisted man.

Queens's Regiment 1779 - 1789, a dragoon, an officer and a mounted dragoon

Queen's Dragoon Regiment

This regiment was raised in 1717. From 1733 – 1763 this was the Queen Fryderyka Regiment, It was converted to infantry in 1776.

Garrisoned: Pomorsze Province 1717, Poznań 1763, Łowic 1775

Chiefs: Maj. Gen. Fryderyk Francuszek Skórzewski, Cupbearer of Lithuania (1726); Francuszek Skórzewski 23 Sept 1759, Lt. Gen. 1761; Maj. Gen. Antoni Czapski Antoni, 10 Dec 1773.

Colonels: Antoni Czapski 23 Sept 1759 until 10 Dec 1773; Karol Manstein (1776).

Prince's Dragoon Regiment

The regiment was formed in 1717. From 1733 – 1763 this was the Prince's Horse Regiment of his Majesty Frederick. In 1789 it became the 8th Infantry regiment under Antoni Czapski.

It was stationed in Pomorski 1717, Poznań (1763), Łowicz (1775)

The Grand Hetman's Horse Regiment

The regiment was formed in 1717. In 1789 it was converted into the 2nd Advanced Guard regiment of the Grand Hetman.

Garrisoned: Lwow County, Province of Wołyń, Bełz, Podlase, Pomerania 1717, Lubomla.

Chiefs: Adam Mikołaj Sieniawski, Governor of Bełz, Grand Hetman of the Crown 30 Apr 1706 until his death 18 Feb 1726; Józef Potocki Governor of Kiev, Grand Hetman of the Crown 9 Nov 1735 until his death in 7 May 1751; Jan Klemens Branicki 5 June 1752 until his death on 9 Oct 1771; Wacłwac Rzewuski 9 Apr 1773 until 16 Mar 1774; Francuszek Kaswery Branicki 8 Feb 1774

Colonels: Maj. Gen. Wilga (1738); Maj Gen. Antoni Granowski, Starosta of Tarnogorski (1754), Lt. Gen.1775 do 1777; Stanisław Łętowski until his death in 1784; Francuszek Puget 8 Apr 1784; Karol Zawojski 1786; Józef Zajączek 1787.

The Field Hetman's Horse Regiment

This regiment was formed in the early 18th century and became the 3rd Advance Guard Regiment in 1789.

Garrisoned: Podhorce, Strzelno 1775, Tetyów 1779

Chiefs: Crown Field Hetman Stanisław Rzewuski 30 Apr 1706, Legal Advisor to the Crown until 1726; Stanisław Chomętowski 11 Oct 1726, Governor of Mazowia until his death on 2 Sept 1728; Jan Klemens Branicki 1735 – 1752; Wacław Rzewuski, Governor of Podolia and then Krakow 1752 – 1773; Francuszek Ksawery Branicki 1773 – 1774; Seweryn Rzewuski 1775 – 1793.

Colonels: Maj Gen. Roch Wieniawski 10 March 1752 (1762); Józef Podhorodeński 21 March 1775 (1789).

Grand Hetman's Dragoon regiment in the 1770's from Raspe. An officer, dragoon and mounted drummer.	Field Hetman's Dragoon regiment in the 1770's. Dragoon in winter off-duty dress, off-duty officer, drummer and dragoon.

Raczyński Foundation Dragon Regiment

The regiment was founded in 1717 as the Podstoli Horse. In 1776 it became a dragoon regiment and in 1789 it became the 9th infantry regiment.

Dismounted in 1776 (Converted into the 9th Infantry Regiment)

Garrisoned: Wielkopolska, Łowicz 1777

Chiefs: The Crown Steward 1717, Hieronim Wielopolski, Crown Equerry (1726), Lt. Gen. 1761; Kazimierz Raczyński, Crown Scribe, from 2 March 1768; Filip Raczyński, Colonel, Starosta of Mieścicki from 28 May 1771, Maj. Gen.

Colonel: Maj. Gen. Gerschow; Karol Otto de Krokow (1768)

Dismounted Dragoon Regiment

The unit was founded in the 1717 and was dismounted in 1776. In 1789 it was converted into the 7th infantry regiment.

Garrisoned: Międzyrzec (1764), Kościan 1775

Chief: Col. Ernest Krysztof Przebendowski 1717; Maj. Gen. Bukowski (1743), Prince Lubormirski Steward of Lithuania 1754; Potocki, Castellan of Bracława, Starosta Trębowela 1755, Lt. Gen. 1761; Joachim Potocki, Cupbearer of the Grand Duchy of Lithuania (1764) until 1.VII.1774; Lt. Gen. Antoni Sułkowski, Governor of Gniezno 1.VII.1774 –1776; Jan Potocki Starosta of Szczerzycki.

Colonel: Mniszek (1743); Maj. Gen Mossakowski (1768); Karol de Pirch (1772), Maj. Gen. 1777.

Battles and Skirmishes: Uprising in the Ukraine, Bar Confederation,

The dismounted Dragoon Regiment of Col Przedbendowski in the 1730's

Crown Cavalry of 1794

Starozakonna Light Cavalry Regiment

This was also known as the Jewish Light Cavalry Regiment (lekkokonny pułk żydowski or the Jewish City Guard). It was formed in 1794 during the Kościuszko Insurrection.

The unit organized in Warsaw and took part in actions at Maciejowice and Praga.

During the 18th century the Jews of Poland were exempted from being conscripted into the Commonwealth's forces. A Jewish merchant in Warsaw name Joseph Aronowicz approached Kosciuszko about forming a Jewish cavalry regiment. The unit was raised in the district of Praga in September-October of 1794 under the command of Colonel Bereck Joselwicz.. This was designated a dragoon unit and eventually reached the size of 500 troopers. For religious reasons the troopers were not required to shave and were nicknamed the "bearded" army (Storozynski, p203). Most of the troopers were killed at Praga.

Volunteer Cavalry of 1794

1794 – One unit of volunteer horse shown by Norbin by wore a green dolman and trousers with black boots. Facings and piping (including pants stripe) were red with yellow buttons. Kiwer was black with white cords and plume. The belting was black.

Peasant cavalry wore long white coats similar to a sukmana and blue pants with a red outer stripe. The belts were black leather. The lance pennants were white over green. The headgear seems to have been black round hats with a green plume on the left side. Both Stachowicz and later Knötel picture them in this dress. The saddle cloth seems to have been white with black piping or blue with red piping.

Hussar Detachment

These Hussars operated in September from Warsaw to Galicia under the command of Major J. Krasicki.

1794 A blue hussar uniform with yellow (ochre) distinctions. Hungarian knots of the front of the pants. Collar, cuffs and lacework is yellow. Hungarian knots above the cuffs. Fifteen brass buttons down the front of the dolman with double lace and knots. The pelisse is ochre with 2 inches of black fur on the cuffs and edging. The pelisse has black lace across the front and on the collar. The sabretache is ochre with dark blue trim with the word "Jednosc" written diagonally across the length. This had white belting.

This unit was formed in August. The drawing is based on drawings from Aleksandra Orlawski. The giwer is black with a green plume. The horse cloth was green with a black stripe.

Uniform of the Krasicki Hussars in the Polish Army Museum (right)

Crown Cavalry Formations during the Uprising of 1794

Baranowski's command operating under the name "3ʳᵈ Regiment of Horse"
Battles and Skirmishes: around Dęblina 27 Aug, Góra 28 Aug, along the Wisła 29 Aug.

The Partisan group of Maj. Białomowski
Part of the Division of Gen. Dąbrowski 18 Oct

Deniski's Command

Frankowski's cavalry detachment
Took part in battles in Mazowia and Podlasie, May - July

Cavalry detachment of horse pikemen
Organized under the command of Vice-brigadier Dąbrowski
Commander: Col. Antoni Gładyszewski
Battles and Skirmishes: Rosławice 22 May

Volunteer Horse Regiment of Col. Kwaśniewski.
This unit was raised prior to 26 Apr and used around Warsaw. It was later converted to infantry.
Battles and Skirmishes: Kolno 7 July, Praga 4 Nov..

Mazurian Horse
Created in June as a detachment of Dąbrowski's Brigade
Battles and Skirmishes: Rosławice 22 May, around Warszaw, Cybulice 8 Aug.

Cavalry detachment of Major Morawski

Ośmiałowski's detachment of Horse
Formed in May in Warszaw

Pągowski's detachment of Horse
Formed in May in Warszaw

Col. Piotrowski's cavalry detachment
Formed in April in Warsaw
Battles and Skirmished: Powązki 28 Aug.

Col. Podhorodeński cavalry detachment

Poniński's cavalry detachment

Lt. Sierpiński's detachment of free Cossacks
Attached to Gen. Zajączak's Division
Battles: Chełm 8 June

Sokoł's Cavalry detachment
Attached to Gen. Zajączak's Division
Battles and Skirmishes: Chełm 8 June, Gołków 9 July.

Col. Toliński's cavalry detachment
Battles and Skirmishes: Nadarzyn 22 Sept, Praga 4 Nov.

Militia Cavalry from the encampment by Stachowski

Technical Corps

Crown Artillery Corps

The Corps was originally formed in 1710 by Marcin Kątski. It was reorganized in 1763 by Alojzy Brühl, who was named General of the Crown Artillery. This was the first reform in the previous sixty years. In 1777 the corps was split into two brigades: Warsaw and Kamieniecz, each of three companies. Each company had 393 soldiers.

1764 – 1789 black tricornes had gold lace, white cockades and white plumes. They had black half boots. Officers had gold buttons and epaulettes. They had long green watch coats with yellow lace edging the cuffs and collar.

Officer – 1790 - Tall black konfederatka with gold band and white plume
1793-94 an NCO's had red pant stripe and gold NCO lace. The headgear was the infantry shako with a traversed white crest. The gunner has white pants with boots and a round hat with red plume.

The Standing Company (Kompanje stojące) was formed in 1764 in Warsaw. The commanders were Józef Gembarzewski, Marjan Dyzmy Pruski and Ernest Ulrych Jaucha.

Commanders: General of the Artillery: Marcin Kątski Castellan of Krakow, died 1710, Jakób Henryk Flemming, Commander lit. 1710 -1712, Jakób Zygmunt Rybiński, Wojewoda of Chełm 1712 – 1725, Jan Stanisław Kątski, kor. 1725 – 1727, Jan Klemens Branicki 1727- 1735, Jan Rybiński Jan, Adjutant Gen of His Majesty the King and the Regiment 1735 – 1737; Prince Aleksander Lubormirski, 1737 –1746, Graf Henryk Brühl Henryk, 1st Minister, Commander of the Saxon Army in Poland 1746 – 1763, Alojzy Fryderyk Brühl, ending in 1763, again 22.XII.1764 until 1788, Szczęsny Potocki 1788 – 1793.

Freikompany created r. 1717, associated with the Artillery Corps in 1767. Commanded by Maj. Pruski 1752-1767.

The Company was stationed in Warsaw in 1764. Commanders: Józef Gembarzewski, Marjan Dyzmy Pruski 1752-1767, Ernest Ulrych Jaucha, Chrystjan Deybel; In Kamieńce: Józef DeWitte, from 12.VII 1764 Potocki.

Company I. Stationed in Kąmieńce, commanders: Capt. Chrystjan Deybel, 1767, Maj. 27 Feb 1772, Maj. Józef DeWitte 1772.

Company II. (from 1773 it was the designated the Vth Company, Garrisoned at Kamieńts) Capt. Chrystjan Dahlke, absent 1 Sept 1769;Józef Witte 1769 to Com. I, Jan 1772;Józef Bedoński to Com. III, 1773; Franciuszek Rexyn 23 Feb 1773.

Company III. (from 1773 it was designated the VIth Company, Garrisoned at Kamieńts) commanded by: Capt. Józef de Witte 1767, vacant 1768; Józef Bedoński 4 Aug 1771, to Com. I; Capt. August Cichocki 18 July 1772, to Comp. II,1773; Józef Bedoński 1773, died 28 Oct 1774,Karol Łoski 15 May 1775.

Company IV (from 1773 it was designated the IIth Company), Garrisoned in Warsaw: Capt. Antoni Konarski 1767 – (1772).

Company V (from 1773 it was designated the IIIrd Company): Capt Chrystjan August d'Aster 1767.

Company VI (from 1773 it was designated IVth Company), Garrisoned in Warsaw: Capt. Antoni Konarski 1767 (1772).

Company V (from 1773 it was designated the IIIrd Company): Capt. Chrystjan August d'Aster 1767.

Company VI (from 1773 it was designated IVth Company) Garrisoned in Warsaw, Capt. Franciszek Rexyn

Crown artillery in 1732. An NCO, a colonel, Freicompany artillery dragon, Fusilier of the artillery

A gunner with a spontoon in 1732. The banner of the Freicompani artillery dragoons

A staff officer in 1778. Officer in everyday dress 1764 - 1775. Gunner in 1775

Crown artillery in 1775 by Raspe

Lithuanian artillery (move) 220

NCO and gunner in 1794

THE ARTILLERY COMPANY IN OCTOBER 1790.

Company – Maj. Gen. Jan Potocki Warsaw,

Company – Lt. Col. Konarski in Warsaw,

Company - Capt. Kapelli in Warsaw,

Company – Col. Deybla in Krakow,

Company - Capt. Dobrski in Wolbroma,

Company - Capt. Górski in Wolbroma,

Company -Maj. Jan Kanto Gembarzewski in Kamienets, (as of 1792 the active army artillery).

Company - Capt. Marszycki in Kamienets,

Company -Capt. Łączyński in Kamienets,

Company –Lt. Col. Łoski in Połonny,

Company –Maj. Napiórkowski in Połonny,

Company - Capt. Falkowski in Połonny,

Company - Capt. Dzierżyński in Tulczyna,

Company - Capt. Aksamitowski w Tulczyna.

THE ARTILLERY COMPANY IN APRIL 1793

Company – Col. Krystjan Gottfryd Deyblin Warsaw, Maj. Gen. 23 May 1794,

Company – Lt. Col. Stanisław Wągrowski in Warsaw,

Company - Maj. Ludwik Dobrski in Warsaw, Col. 23 May 1794

Company - Capt. Karola Szubalskiego in Warsaw, Lt. Col. 23 May 1794

Company - Capt. Moszczyński in Warsaw, killed 17 April 1794

Company - Lt. Col. Łoski in Kamienets, taken into the Russian army or killed

Company -Maj. Gembarzewski in Kamienets taken into the Russian army or killed,

Company - Capt. Marszycki in Kamienets taken into the Russian army or killed,

Company - Capt. Łączyński in Kamienets taken into the Russian army or killed,

Company – Lt. Col. Konarski in Krasno, Col. 1794, taken into the Russian army of killed,

Company – Lt. Col. Napiórski in Krasno, taken into the Russian army or killed,

Company -Capt. Aksamitowski in Krasno, taken into the Russian army or killed,

Company - Capt. Antoni Pierściński in Krasno, Maj. 23 May 1794, taken into the Russian Army or killed,

Company - Maj. Józef Górski in Szarogrodna, Col. 18 May 1794, taken into the Russian army of killed,

Company - Capt. Magieryin Szarogrodna, taken into the Russian army or killed,

Company -Capt. Mirosławski in Szarogrodna, taken into the Russian army or killed,

Uniform of a Crown Artillery officer 1789 - 1794

Crown Engineer Corps

The corps was formed by the Sejm in 1775 under the overall command of the Corps of Artillery. In 1791 they organized a company of pioneers under the Engineering Corps.

1772 – 1789 Conductors had gold lace on the collar, cuffs and lapels. They wore black hats with gold lace, white cockades and black boots. Officers had gold epaulettes.

1790 – 1794 Engineering troops included sappers. They are pictured with a regulation infantry casquet with brass plat and white plume. Officers wore a dark green konfederatka with gold central band and white head band. They also had white cords and plume.

Chief: Alojzy Fryderyk Brühl, General of the Artillery

Colonels: Lt. Col. Jan Klein (1786), Karol Sierakowski 1789.

A military engineer in 1732, blue-grey coat and vest, navy blue pants. Gunner in black hat with yellow braid, green coat, vest and pants, red turnbacks. Train driver, black hat, green coat and pants.

Conductor and engineer officer in 1775. In another copy of Raspe the black is replaced by purple.

Officers of the crown engineers in 1790.

Sappers in 1790. Sapper in summer uniform, NCO of the miners, a sapper.

Crown Pontoniers Corps

The Pontoniers Corps was formed from militia companies in 1764. Until 1776 the officers were appointed by the war commission. From 1777 these appointments were made by the king.

The pioneers were stationed in Warsaw and Praga, then in Nieszawa and Nowi Dworza. At the time of the Kosciuszko Insurrection the Pioneers were organized into the 16th Infantry regiment.

Left to right, Officer of the pontoneers in 1775, An officer in the Skarbowy Militia, a solider of the pnotooners. An officer in daily dress.

CROWN MILITIA

Created from individual units by Crown Treasurer Wessel in 1767. It was under the command of the Crown Treasury Commission, consisting of infantry and cavalry units from the Ukrainian, Ruthenian and Wielkopolski. From 1791 it consisted only of infantry.

Pontonier Battalion (Part of the Crown Militia)

Royal militia hussars based on a painting of Stanislaus Poniatowski passing in Krakow, 1791

Court soldier, a Court militia officer and an officer in the livery of the court chamberlin. BG indicates the uniforms were yellow wiht navy blue distinctions

Army of The Grand Duchy of Lithuania

Lithuanian Infantry

Guard Regiment of Infantry Grand Duchy of Lithuania

The regiment was stationed in Wilno.
The regiment had one battalion of eight companies, one of which was a grenadier company.

1770 – 1789 Grenadiers had brown bearskins with brass front plates and red plumes. Grenadiers wore brass mitres with white plumes.

1790 – 1794 - pants had gold lace on the thighs in Hungarian fashion. The soldiers and officers wore a side to side bicorne in black with gold lace and black plumes. The grenadiers wore brown bearskins with no visor and brass front plate and white cords.

Garrisoned: Warszaw, Wilno
Chief: Gultz 1717; Gen. Flemming, Swordbearer of the Grand Duchy of Lithuania (1759); Prince Adam Czartoryski Adam, General, Lord of Podolska 1775; Prince Stanisław Jabłonowski, Maj. Gen. 1784; Ignacy Tyzenhauz Ignacy 1793;
Colonels: Franzeszek Szyldebach (Schielbach) 22 Jan1770; Jan Deskur 20 July 1774
The regiment was absorbed into the Russian Army 15 April 1794

The miter of the Lithuanian Guard from the 1730's.

A staff officer in 1775, Lt Gen Adam Czartoryski, head of the regiment 1779 - 1783, a grenadier in summer uniform 1770 and a grenadier in 1775

Officer in 1792 uniform by Jozef Harasimowicz

A soldier, officer and grenadier in 1792 based on Harasimowisz

Grenadier in 1792 uniform by Jozef Harasimowicz

1st Regiment of Infantry of the Grand Hetman of Lithuania

The regiment was formed in 1717 as The Infantry Regiment of the Grand Hetman of the Grand Duchy of Lithuania. In 1776 it was the 1st Grenadier regiment. Later it became the 1st Grand Hetman of the Grand Duchy of Lithuania's Infantry regiment.

Garrisoned: Borysów (1777), Słonim 1783 – 1792, Wiłkomierz Dec 1792.
Chief: The Grand Hetman of the Grand Duchy of Lithuania: Prince Michał Wiśniowiecki, 1735 until his death in 1744; Prince Michał Kazimirz Rybeńko Radziwiłł until his death in 1762; Prince Michał Massalski until his death 1768; Michał Ogiński 1768 do 1793, Szymon Kossakowski 1793.
Colonels: Gen. Sokół 1717; Prince Radziwiłł; Col. Miecznik (1754 – 1759), Lt. Gen Rzewuski, (1762), Col. Oskierko (1766);Józef Pac 18 Sept 1776;Ignacy Rymiński 22 Dec 1783, Morawski 1790

Battles and Skirmishes:1792 Mir 11 June;**1794** Sałaty 29 July, Wilno 11 Aug.

1775 – 1789 White pompoms on a black hat with white lace and gold distinctions and buttons

1792 Officer of the rifle unit is pictured with red turnbacks, lapels and collar. The pants had a red stripe down the side. All leatherwork was white. The shoulder strap was red. The Shako was black with a gold band, white cords and white plume. Enlisted wore black leather belts

The regiment fought in the 1792 war against Russia.
182

1775, soldier and officer of the 1st Grand Hetman Regiment, officer and soldier of the 2nd Grand Hetman Regiment

Rifleman of the 1st Grand Hetman regiment in 1792 by Harasimowicz

(below left) 1792, soldier of 1st Grand Hetman in a dark blue uniform with orange facings, gold buttons, black hat with brass fittings. Officer of the second Grand Hetman Regiment in navy cap with silver lace nd white bow, navy blue pants, silver buttons and crimson/siler sash. An officer of the rifles in a green uniform with red facings, brass metal, crimson/silver sash. Rifleman same colors as above.

(Right) Officer of the riflemen of the 1st Grand Hetman Regiment in 1792 by Harasimowicz

2nd Regiment of Infantry of the Grand Hetman of Lithuania

Thus unit was formed in 1775 from the Grand Hetman's Dragoon Regiment
Garrisoned: Grodno, Sokółka 1792
Chief: Michał Ogiński, Grand Hetman of the Grand Duchy of Lithuania 1775 - 1793
Colonels: Ignacy Morawski 4.X.1775, Grzegorz Wolan 9.I.1784, Karol Morawski 25.V.1789
Battles and Skirmishes:1792 Mir 11 June, Breść 23 July.

1775 – 1789 – the grenadier company had a white metal mitre.
1790 - 1792 - the jacket had pointed cuffs. Officers wore a blue konfederatka with white band and plume.

(Left) Officer of the 3rd Field Hetman's Regiment in 1775 based on Raspe. An officer of the 4th Field Hetman's Regiment. Infantryman of the 3rd Field Hetman and the 4th Field Hetman's Regiment

(Right) A soldier and officer of the 2nd Grand Hetman's Regiment in 1789. Private of the 3rd Field Hetman's Regiment. Private of the 4th Field Hetman's Regiment

3rd Regiment of Infantry of the Field Hetman of Lithuania

Formed in 1717 as the Infantry Pułk of the Field Hetman of Lithuania, about 1759 it was called the infantry regiment of the Field Hetman of the Grand Duchy of Lithuania. Around 1776 it was called the 3rd Regiment of the Field Hetman of the Grand Duchy of Lithuania. In 1793 it became the 3rd Lithuanian Regiment.

Garrisoned: Mińsk (1775), Janiszki 1778, Nowogródek, Szereszów (1778) – 1789, Kowno 1789, Wilno 1790, Kowno 1791, Preny Dec.1792, Szaty 1794.

Chief: The Field Hetman of Lithuania: Stanisław Miecznik Denhoff until his death 1728; Prince Michał Rybeńko Radziwiłł from 1736 – 1744; Michał Józef Massalski 4.X.1744 until 1762, Aleksander Michał Sapieha 1762, Józef Sosnowski Wojewod of. Połocki 1776 do 1780; Ludwig Tyszkiewicz 1780 – 1793; Kossakowski, Secretary Crown 1794.

Colonels: Brzostowski, Starosta Orszański (1754) Lt. Gen. (1755); Józef Osipowski 13.II.1778, near Smoleńsk 1787; Prince Ignacy Giedroyć (1789); Pawel Grabowski 1794.

Battles and Skirmishes: 1792 Granne 24 July; 1794 Wilno 11 Aug, Praga 4 Nov

A private of the 3rd Field Hetman's Regiment in 1792 by Harasimowicz

Soldiers of 3rd Lithuanian Infantry Regiment in 1792.

4th Regiment of Infantry of the Field Hetman of Lithuania

Formed in 1775 from the Field Hetman of the Grand Duchy of Lithuania's Horse (Dragoon) Regiment.

Garrisoned: Brześć, Terespol 1783, Wilno (1787 – 1789), Borysów 1790, Mińsk 1791, Słuck 1792, Żyżmory 1794.
Chief: The Field Hetman of the Grand Duchy of Lithuania, Józef Sosnowski, Wojewoda Połock 1776 – 1780; Ludwig Tyszkiewicz 1780 – 1793; Kossakowski.
Colonels: Adam Papłoński 3 Aug 1776 – 1790; Jan Meyen 30 Nov 1790
Battles and Skirmishes: 1792 Mir 11 July; **1794** Wilno 22/23 Apr, Praga 4 Nov.

5th Regiment Lithuanian Infantry of Paul George Grabowski

The regiment was formed 30 April 1775 under the name Royal Dragon Regiment of the Grand Duchy of Lithuania.

1790 – 1792 Skirts were dark blue with light blue lace and pant stripe.

Garrisoned: Pińsk, Wilno 1778, Mścibów 1779, Wilno 1783, Brześć Litewski 1789

Chiefs: Michał Grabowski, Inspector General. 24 Oct 1775 – 1783; Paweł Jerzy Grabowski 30 Dec 1783, killed 4 Oct 1794.

Colonels: Jerzy Grabowski 16 Dec 1776 – 24 Oct 1783, Maciej Frankowski 30 Aug 1783, Rafał Berken 1794.

Battles and Skirmishes: 1792 - Mir 11 July, Brześć 23 July; **1794** Soły 25 June, Praga 4 Nov.

(Left) Soldier 5th Regiment 1775, soldier 6th Regiment. Officer 5th Regiment and 6th regiment.

(Right) Soldiers of the 5th and 6th regiment in 1792 and officers of the same.

6th Regiment Lithuanian Infantry of Xavier Niesiołowski

The unit was formed in 1775

Garrisoned: Wilno, Nowogródek 1790, Poniewiecz 1792.
Chiefs: Prince Ksawery Massalski 4.V.1775, Ksawet Niesiołowski, Wojewode of Nowogrodzki 1785
Colonels: Belcour Thesby. 2 Mar 1781, Kazimierz 1794.
Battles and Skirmishes: 1792 - Mir 11 June, Brześć 23 July; **1794** Sałaty 29 July.

1775 – 1789 A picture of a grenadier shows a brass mitre with red backing. A 1783 image shows the jacket closed with no lapels.
1792 Officers had yellow pant stripe. Konfederatka with yellow band, white edges cords and plume. The belts were black Leather. Front skirts dark blue with yellow edging.

The regiment fought in the 1792 war against Russia.

A grenadier of the 6th Regiment in 1783 in summer dress. The collar, cuffs and turnbacks are crimson. A general in charge of the foot guards in 1777, red jacket with dark blue distinctions. Gold distinctions and crimson sash. Officer in off-duty dress, black hat with gold braid, crimson uniform, gold buttons, 1770.

Officer of the 6th regiment in 1794 by Jozef Harasimowicz

7th Regiment Lithuanian Infantry of Prince Kazimierz Nestor Sapiehia

This regiment was formed from several independent companies that became the Grodno Battalion in 1790, during the long sejm and participated in the War against Russia. They were also called "fizyliers".

Garrisoned: Oszmiańskie, Wilno 1791, Smorgonie 1791, Oszmiana 1792, Wilno, Smorgonie 1791, Oszmiana 1792, Wilno, Smorgonie 1794.
Chief: Kazimierz Nestor Sapieha, Gen, of the Artillery and Chief of the Engineer Corps, Ludwig Giełgud, Strażnik W. Ks. Lit. 1793 – 1794.
Colonels: Feliks Gorzeński, Lt. Col. Stafan Grabowski (1791) – 1794.

Battles and Skirmishes: 1792 - Brześć 23 July; **1794** - Wilno 22/23 Apr , Soły 25 June, Praga 4 Nov.

8th Regiment Lithuanian Infantry of the House of Radziwiłł

Formed 1 Mar 1790 as a regiment from the Radziwiłł Estate, disbanded in January 1794 and re-formed in April 1794.

Garrisoned: Nieśwież 1792, Czarnobyl 1791, Nieśwież 1792, Płońsk, Stwołowicze 1793.
Chiefs: Prince Karol Radziwiłł, Wojewoda Wilno, Lt. Gen. 17 Sept 1789, died 1790; Seweryn Rzewuski.
Colonels: Prince Michał Radziwiłł;Lt. Col. Seweryn Rzewuski 1 Mar 1790; Dominik Dederko.
Battles and Skirmishes: 1792 Mir 11 June, Zelwa 4 July, Załuże 11 July, Brześć 23 Aug; **1794** Soły 25 June.

1790 – 1794 round cuffs. Officer's konfederatka was dark blue with white piping and band. White cords and plume. The hat band was brown.

9th Regiment Lithuanian Infantry

The regiment was formed in 1794 at the time of the Kosciuszko Insurrection

Grand Hetman of Lithuania's Rifleman Hungarian Company

The company was in existence from 1717 – 1793. It was nominally under command of the Grand Hetman of Lithuania.

Chief: The Grand Hetman of the Grand Duchy of Lithuania 1717 – 1793
Commanders: Capt. Oborski (1787); Col. Suchodolski (1789); Capt. Felicjan Bontani (1792).
Garrisoned: Near the Grand Hetman of the Grand Duchy of Lithuania

They were dress as the Crown Hungarian companies, but with yellow facings.

Field Hetman of Lithuania's Hungarian Company

The Hungarian Company of the Field Hetman were considered Grenadiers of the army. They were in existence from 1717 to 1793.

Chief: The Field Hetman of the Grand Duchy of Lithuania from 1717
Rotmistrz: Jerzy Grzymała do 29 June 1778; Jan Liebe 29 June1778.
Garrisoned: Near the Field Hetman of the Grand Duchy of Lithuania

Court of Justice of Lithuania's Hungarian Company

Garrisoned: Mejszagoła I Szyrwinty Dec 1792.

Grand Marshal of Lithuania's Hungarian Company

This elite company was in the service of the Republic from 1717 until 1794.

Chief: The Mashal of the Grand Duchy of Lithuania
Rotmistrz: Onufry Zawadzki (1787), Józef Grzymała Lubański (1793).

The Grand Hetman of Lithuania's Janissary Company

This unit was stationed wherever the Grand Hetman was encamped.

Chief: The Grand Hetman of the Grand Duchy of Lithuania
Rotmistrz: Jan Bułhak; Lachnicki Ignacy 7 May 1780, mjr. after 8 Dec of that year; Stokowski 8 Dec 1780

The Field Hetman of Lithuania's Janissary Company

The unit was stationed wherever the Field Hetman was encamped.

Chief: The Field Hetman of the Grand Duchy of Lithuania
Rotmistrz: Antoni Tołoczko (1751)

(Top left) Janissaries from 1770 - two soldiers and an officer.

(Top right) Grand Hetman's Company. A soldier in 1775 and an officer from 1770.

(Bottom left) Officer of Field Hetman's Janissaries - White turban, green vest and hat, black edging, silver braid and red pants, white zupan and yellow shoes. Jannissary in the same dress as above with red strips and gold embelishments, black shoes. Janissary with pale jacket with white zuppan, crimson distinctions and black shoes

INFANTRY FROM THE GRAND DUCHY OF LITHUANIA DURING THE 1794 UPRISING

Light Infantry from the Bielski area, Commanded by Maj. Cetys
  Skirmishes: at Lachowa 1 July.

Battalion of Scythemen, commanded by Dauksza

Militia of Grodno, formed 25 May, under the command of Ehrenkreutz

Light Infantry Battalion, under the command of Grabiński
  Battles and Skirmishes: Soły 25 June, Praga 4 Nov

Volunteers, under the command of Horodeński, formed in June

The Grodno Corps, under the command of Maj. Gen. Constantine Jelski

Scythemen of Wiłkomirsca, under the command of Komar
  Battles and Skirmishes: Poszołoty 10 July, Praga 4 Nov

The Bresc-Litowsk Battalion, commanded by Lt. Col. Kulesza
  Battle: at Krupczyca 16 Sept

Lissowski's Detachment

Courland Uprising, commanded by Maj. Gen. Mirbach, formed 27 June.

Free Light Infantry, commanded by Michał Ogiński, then after that Morykoni,
  Battles and Skirmishes: Wołożyn 15 June, at Iwienic 19 June

Kowieński's Light Infantry Battalion, commanded by Maj. Gen. Prozor
  Skirmishes: Szemberk 3 June, Radziwiliszki 12 June

Bielsk pikemen, commanded by Maj. Roltzberg,
Skirmish: Stawiska 3 July.

Kobryńsc Light Infantry, commanded by Maj. Gen. Kazimierz Ruszczyc.

Wileńsciand Upitsci Light Infantry, commanded by Capt. Saczkiewicz,
Skirmish: at Sałata 29 July.

Prince Kazimierz Saphieha Light Infantry, commanded Giejsztor

Grodno Light Infantry, commanded by Col. Sochacki, around Praga 4 Nov.

Szawelscy Riflemen, commanded by Maj. Gen. Stetkiewicz,
  Skirmishes: at Zagóra 22 June.

Grodno Light Infantry, commanded by Col. Michał Trębicki, Fought around Praga 4 Nov.

Rosieńsci Light Infantry, commanded by Maj. Gen Michał Tyszkiewicz

The Wilno Municipal Guard, formed in May

Telszewski Uprising, commanded by Maj. Gen. Wojtkiewicz

Light Infantry, commanded by Lt. Col. Wolan, fought around Praga 4 Nov

Insurgent Militia of Wołkowyski, fought around Praga 4 Nov

Prince Żmudzki's Light Infantry

Lithuanian Cavalry

Horse Guards Regiment of the Grand Duchy of Lithuania

The Horse Guards were formed in 1717 as a Dragoon regiment. It was originally titled as the Lejbregiment Dragonów Królewskich Wielkiego Księstwa Litewskiego(Guard Dragoons of the Grand Duchy of Lithuania). From 1762 it was known as Regiment Konny Króla Imci Wielkiego Księstwa Litewskiego (King's Regiment of Horse of the Grand Duchy of Lithuania), from 1784 it was the Regiment Gwardii Konnej Wielkiego Księstwa Litewskiego (Guard Horse Regiment of the Grand Duchy of Lithuania), and from 1793 it was titled Regiment Karabinierów Gwardii Konnej Litewskiej (Guard Regiment of Carabiners of the Grand Duchy of Lithuania).

Garrisoned: Grodno, Prużany (1783) - 1792
Chiefs: Gen. Sapieha 1717; Prince, Gen. Radziwiłł, Exchequer of the Grand Duchy of Lithuania 1755; Prince Lt. Gen. Stanisław Ignacy Radziwiłł, Chamberlain of the Grand Duchy of Lithuania (1759 – 1764); Maj. Gen Grabowski (1765 – 1786); Prince Mikołaj Radziwiłł (1786 – 1790), Jan Strjeński 1792.
Colonels: Prince Mikołaj Radziwiłł Mikołaj until 1786; Jerzy Obryn 1786; Krysztof Engelhardt (1792).
Battles and Skirmishes: Bar Confederation, Widawa

1792 - gold epaulettes. Black side to side bicorne with gold lace and white plume

Trooper and officer in 1775. An officer in 1792

Guard Dragoon officer in 1792 by Harasimowicz

1st Brigade National Cavalry of the Grand Duchy of Lithuania, so-called Hussars of Kowieńska

Formed in 1776 from the Kaunas Hussars

Stationed: Kaunas, Mińsk (1789), Kiejdany (1790), Wiłkomierz, Poniewież, Rosienie, Szawle.
Commanders: Kazimierz Tyszkiewicz, Lt. Gen. from 1778;Tadeusz Puzyna, Maj.Gen. in 3 July 1778; Szymon Zabiełło 26 June 1788;Mikołaj Sulistrowski (1791); Frankowski (1792)
Battles and Skirmishes: 1792 - Świerzeń 10 June, Mir 11 June, Johaniszkiele. 1794 - Brześć 23 July, Szczucin 13 May, Poniewież 20 May, Szkudy 12 July.

1776 – 1785 Towarzysz had a red kuczma with black band and a red plume. They wore a red sash. The pocztowy had a black busby with a red plume and bag. All ranks had a white cockade.

1st Brigade, 1776 - 1789. An officer, Towarzycz and a Pocztowy

1st Brigade in 1792. An officer with a scarlet cap and distinctions, white cords and plume, navy blue uniform, crimson stripes on pants, gold buttons and epaulettes. Trooper with same uniform. Lance and penant blue over magenta. The third figure is a Towarzycz of the 2nd brigade in the same colors.

2nd Brigade National Cavalry of the Grand Duchy of Lithuania, so-called Ligth Horse of Pinsk

Formed in 1776 from the Petyhorski of Pińsk.

Garrisoned: In and around Pińsk.
Commanders: Ksawery Chomiński, the Strarosta of Pińsk; Piotr Antoni Twardowski 14.X.1790;
Józef Kopeć 1794
Battles and Skirmishes: 1792 - Mir 11 June - Dubienka 18 May. 1794 - Mikołajów 23 May,
around Warszaw, Gołchów 9 July, Wola 27 July, Wilno 10 Aug, Swedish Battery 25 Aug, Powązki
28 Aug, Błonie 9 Sept, Maciejowice 10 Oct, Praga 4 Nov

1764 – 1776 The Petyhorski cavalry in Lithuania, (the equivalent of medium cavalry or dragoons).
The headdress for ordinary soldiers was a tall felt or wool cap vertically quilted czapka. Officers
wore a more traditional konfederatka. Some officers still wore breastplates.

1776 – 1785 Officers had a blue/grey kontusz and a yellow konfederatka with a white cockade,
white plume and yellow boots. The pocztowy wore a black busby with a black plume. All wore
yellow pants with a blue stripe and cuffs.

1792 the towarzysz is depicted in a shako with front visor upturned. The lances were striped in
the colors of the lance pennant

Petychorski in 1752 - a lieutenant of a squadron.
Pocztowy in 1746. An officer of the Pancerni in 1764.

Petychorski in 1785. An officer, Towarzycz and
Pocztowy. BG says that navy with crimson was the
norm, however blue and yellow flags were prescribed
for the advance guard units since 1746.

Trumpeter in Duchy National Cavalry. Black giwer with white cords and a blue tassel. Crimson jacket with navy blue facings. Lace white and navy blue. Trumpet brass. Pocztowy of national cavalry, black giwer, white cords and plume. Navy jacket, crimson facings and white stripes on the trousers. Navy blue saddle cloth with magenta and white stripes.

Towarycz of the Crown Advance Guard in 1785. Parade dress, summer dress and Lituanian troops. The long coat was known as the "Litwika" during the Napoleonic Wars.

3rd Brigade National Cavalry of the Grand Duchy of Lithuania

Formed in 1792

Garrisoned: Rosiena.
Commander: Józef Kossakowski.
Battles and Skirmishes: 1794 - Wilno 11 Aug.

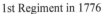

1st Regiment in 1776

1st Regiment according to Rasper, 1776

1st Regiment Advance Guard JKM Grand Duchy of Lithuania Michael Kirkor

This was formed in 1789 from the Dragoon Regiment of Maj. Gen. Szdłowskiego. The regiment was formed in 1776 as light uhlans. It was later absorbed into the Russian army as the Lithuanian-Tartar Regiment.

Garrisoned: Onikszty, Rzeczyca (1789), Chołopienicze (1790).
Colonels: Mustafa Baranowski 12 Oct 1746 (1785); Michał Kirkor (1792)
Battles and Skirmishes: 1792 - Opsa 22 May, Mścibów 10 July, Wojszki 14 July.

1776 – 1790 the pants were yellow with white side stripes. Towarzysz wore black boots and other ranks wore yellow half boots. Officers had white plumes, troopers wore yellow. Towarzysz had yellow belts, pocztowy had white.

2nd Regiment Advance Guard Grand Hetman of Lithuania Josef Jeleński

Formed in 1776 from light cavalry banners

Garrisoned: Borysów, Mozyr (1789), Marjampol (1790), Wiłkomierz, Onikszty (X.1792).
Colonels: Józef Jeleński (1785); August Kadłubiński (1794).
Battles and Skirmishes: Praga 4 Nov 1794

1776 – 1789 Officers had silver epaulettes, troopers had no shoulder straps. Towarzysz had red belts. Officers wore a red konfederatka with a white cockade and plume.

2nd Regiment in 1776. An officer, Towarzysz and Pocztowy based on Raspe

3rd Regiment in 1776. Pocztowy, officer and Towarzycz based on Raspe

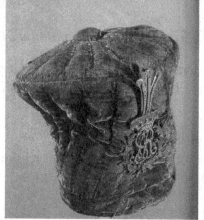

Cap of a Towarzysz 3th Advance Guard GDL 1764 - 1789. PAM

3rd Regiment Advance Guard Field Hetman of Lithuania Antony Chlewińskiego

Formed in 1776 from light cavalry banners

Garrisoned: Mozyr, Łojów (1789), Mozyr (1790), Strzeszyn 1791, Wiłkowyszki (X.1792).
Colonels: Kazimierz Romanowski (1785); Maj. Gen. Antoni Chlewiński; Piruski
Battles and Skirmishes:1792 - Zelwa 4 Aug. 1794 - Krupczyce 16 Sept, Breść 17 Sept, Maciejowice 10 Oct, Praga 4 Nov.

1776 – 1789 Plume holder in the National Army Museum is enameled yellow metal with the king's initials (turquoise), crown (blue and gold), wreath (blue with red ribbons) and metal feathers (turquoise and red). Troopers had blue shoulder straps on the left side. Towarzysz had blue belts. Officers wore a blue konfederatka with a white cockade and plume.

4th Regiment in 1775 according to Raspe

Towarzycz and Pocztowy in 1775

Cap of a Towarzysz 4th Advance Guard GDL 1764 - 1789. PAM

4th Regiment Lithuanian Advance Guard of Josef Bielaki

This unit was formed in 1733 from the Tartar banners of the lands of the Potocki, Governors of Kiev. They were transferred from the Saxon Army to the Polish Commonwealth in 1764.

Garrisoned: Kamieniec Lithuania (1782 – 87), Borysów (1790)
Colonels: Sichodziński 1733; Maj. Gen. Murza Rudnicki Czymbaj 1756; Maj. Gen. Józef Bielak 17.IV.1764, until his death in 1794; Mustafa Achmatowicz 1794.
Battles and Skirmishes: The Seven Years War; 1792 - Świerzeń 10 June, Mir 11 June, Zelwa 4 July, Izabelin 7 July, Mścibów 10 July, Brześć 23 July. 1794 - Dereczyn, Maciejowice 10 Oct, Praga 4 Nov.

1776 – 1789 the towarzycz had a red belt. The officers had white plumes, towarzycz had red plumes and all had white cockades. Belting was white; scabbards were black leathers with brass bindings.

199

| Uhlan-Tartar Cavalry in the 18th century. |

The 5th Regiment in 1775. A Pocztowy, officer and Towarzycz based on Raspe

5th Regiment Lithuanian Advance Guard Stanislaw Byszewski

This unit was formed in 1733 from the Tartar banners of the lands of the Potocki, Governors of Kiev. They were transferred from the Saxon Army to the Polish Commonwealth in 1764.

Garrisoned: Suchowola (1772), Krynki (1789), Wielona (X.1792).
Colonels: Hallaszewicz; A. M. Korycki; Gorycz (1785);Maj. Gen. Stanisław Byszewski (1789 – 1792);Ludwig Lissowski
Battles and Skirmishes: The Seven Year's War, Praga 2 Nov.1794.

1764 – 1789 the officers wore a green vest with gold lace. The officers and towarzycz wore white feathers and all wore a white cockade. The towarzycz wore a green belt/sash.

200

6th Regiment of the Advance Guard of the Grand Duchy of Lithuania

Also known as the Tartar Regiment of Jacob Azulewicz - King's Militia and the 2nd Regiment of Nadwórna Ulans. Formed from the 2nd King's Lancers and Commonwealth Light Cavalry, or Uhlans (Tartars) of the Crown Lands in May 1792.

Garrisoned: Kobryń, Łomna (Dec 1792)
Colonels: Jakób Azulewicz died 11 Aug 1794; Achmatowicz.
Battles and Skirmishes: Wilno 11 Aug 1794 r.

Tarter Regiment in 1790. Cap band is black sheeps wool, crimson top and white cords and plume. Navy blue uniform with crimson distinctions and pants. Saddle cloth is crimson and white stripes. Cavalry officer in a blue kontusz with crimson distinctions. Yellow buttonsand gold straps. Silver and crimson sash with yellow boots. Brigadier from 1792 in color similar to the previous with white stripes on the pants. A Brigadier on the 1st Lithuanian Brigade, 1792 - 1794. Same uniform as previous

Tartar Regiment of Alexander Ulano

This unit was also known as the 7th Regiment of Tartars of the Grand Duchy of Lithuania. It was formed in May 1792, by October 1792 it was transferred to the Targowica forces.

Garrisoned: Janów
Colonel: Aleksander Mustafa Ułan

1792 – Red czapka with black lamb's wool band and white plume. There was one white epaulette on the left shoulder. The saddle cloth was red with a white stripe.

8th Regiment of Cavalry of the Grand Duchy of Lithuania

The regiment was formed in 1794 by General Karwowski.

Garrisoned: Wizna
Commander: Maj. Józef Weyssenhoff
Battles and Skirmishes: Magnuszew

Dragoons in the Grand Duchy of Lithuanian Army

His Majesty the Crown Prince's Dragoon Regiment of the Grand Duchy of Lithuania

Dismounted on 30.IV.1775, later becoming the 5th Infantry Regiment of the Grand Duchy.
Garrisoned: Pińsk
Chief: Gen. Ogiński, Field Scribe of the Grand Duchy of Lithuania 1717- 1762.

The Cavalry regiment of the Grand Hetman of Lithuania

The regiment was dismounted in 1775, returned under the name of the 2nd Infantry Regiment – the Grand Hetman of the Grand Duchy of Lithuania
Chief: Grand Hetman Ludwick Pociej Ludwick from 1717 until his death 3.I.1730; Prince Michał Wiśniowiecki, 1735 until his death 1744; Prince Michał [Rybeńko]Radziwiłł, until his death in 1762; Michał Massalski until his death in 1768; Michał Ogiński 1768 – 1775.
Colonels: Kopeć 1717, Jabłonski (1754 – 1759)

The Cavalry regiment of the Field Hetman of the Grand Duchy of Lithuania

The regiment was dismounted in 1775, it returned under the name of the 4th Infantry Regiment – the Field Hetman's of the Grand Duchy of Lithuania.
Chiefs: Field Hetman Michał Denhoff, Swordbearer of the Grand Duchy of Lithuania 1717 until his death on 2 Aug 1728; Prince Michał Radziwiłł 4 Oct 1744 to 1762;Aleksander Michał Sapieha 1762.
Colonels: Oltym 1717; Massalski, Cupbearer of Lithuania and Starosta of Radoszki (1754 – 1759); Fransezek Bitowt (1772).

Field Hetman's Dragoons in 1775 by Raspe. All Dragoons had green jackets.

Army Technicians

Lithuanian Corps of Artillery (Korpus Artylerii Litewskiej)

The Commanders of the Corps were Generals Branicki (1768) and Kazimierz Saphieha 1773.

The Company of Cannoniers was stationed in Wilno (1773). The commanders were Captain Montresor (1773), Marcin Wołk (1774) and Captain Vietynghoff (1779, later promoted to Major 1787).

1775 – 1789 the black tricornes had gold lace with white cockades.

1792 the unit had black leatherwork with gold epaulettes. Some officers wore a dark green letwika with black collar and cuffs. When konfederatka was worn it was with a dark green top, a white band and black lamb's wool band. Comb helmet black with gold band and black plume. Pants were dark green with a black side stripe.

Generals of the artillery are pictured in a high crowned hat with the left side turned up and fixed with a white cockade and plume. There was a gold band. The plumes and lace are sometimes depicted as red.

Lithuanian Artillery in 1775 by Raspe

Lithuanian artilleryin 1789, green coat with black facings and crimson belt. An officer with white band, cords and plume and silver epaulettes.Officer in parade dress. This color scheme would carry over into the Grand Duchy of Warsaw

Bombardier in 1792 by Jozef Harasimowicz

The Standing Company from 1790

Company General: Staff Capt Wincenty Haciski 1 January 1790 – 1793.
Company Colonel: Staff Capt. Kazimierz Miłosz 21 January 1790, Staff Capt Wojciech Wilczewski 19 June 1790,

Company 1st Major: Maj. Jan Vietynghoffa 4 Jan 1784;Capt. Franciszek Michałowski 15 January 1784, Staff Capt. Jan Kublicki 2 November 1790,
Company 2nd Major Francuiszek Józef Mehlera 1790, Staff Capt. Józef Billewicz 19 June,
Company 1st Capt Jan Chrzanowskiego 7 September 1776, Maj. 19 June 1792, Capt. Hjacynta Drozdowski 19 June 1792
Company 2nd Capt. Aleksander Stankara 13 March 1784,
Company 3rd Capt. Jan Au 22 January 1790,
Company 4th Capt. Mikołaj Spensberger 26 May 1790.

Artillery in 1792. Black helmet with with cords and plumes. Green jackets with black distinctions. Silver and crimson sash. An officer, bombardier and gunner. Gunner's pants were green with a black stripe.

Lithuanian officer in 1792 by Jozef Harasimowicz

(Left) Gunner of the Frei-
company Grenadier in 1774.
Grenadier officer in 1775 and
Grenadier Gunner.
(Right) Freicompany Grena-
dier by Raspe in 1775.

The Free Company of Grenadiers was stationed in Wilno (1773). The commanders were Captain Freyderyk Wilhielm Cronenmann (1773, promoted to Lt. Colonel in 1781) and Captain Antoni Godin (1781).

1770 – 1789 the Friekompanie grenadiers wore a brass mitre with red backing. They had green coats and vests with red lapels, cuffs and turnbacks. The gunners wore brass mitres with red backs. They had green coats with black cuffs and lapels and black turnbacks. They had white vests

Generals: Sołłohub; Starosta Jeierzyński, (1754); Potocki; Starosta Tłomacki (1759 – 1762); Branicki, łowcza kor. (1768); Sapieha Kazimierz 22 May 1773
Colonels: Massalski, star. Radoszkowski, (1754), Tadeusz Stetkiewicz 22 May 1773, Fry-deryk Wilhielm Cronenmann 16 Dec 1783, Maj. Gen. 7 August 1792; Kajetan Kosielski 7 July 1792;Jakób Jasiński killed 4 Nov 1794

Engineer Corps of the Grand Duchy of Lithuania

The engineers' corps was first formed in the late 18th century and took part in the Kosciuszko In-surrection.

The Chief of the Corps was also the General of the Artillery,

Chief: Kazimierz Sapieha, General of the Artillery.
Colonel: Jakób Jasiński, killed 4 November 1794

CAVALRY FORMATIONS OF THE GRAND DUCHY OF LITHUANIA DURING THE UPRISING OF 1794

The Grodzieński Cavalry Regiment of Col. Andrzej Kazanowski

Formed in May at Sokółce.
Commander: Col. Andrzej Kazanowski
Battles: Krupczyce 16 Oct. Brześć 17 Sept. Maciejowice 10 Oct

Wilno Cavalry

Formed in June.
Commander: Maj. Gen. Tadeusz Korsak
Battles and Skirmishes: Along the Iwieniec 19 June, around Wilna 19 and 20 July.

Kowieński's Cavalry Unit

Pomeranian Cavalry

Commander: Kruszyński

Lissowski's Regiment of Cavalry

Volunteer Tartar Cavalry Troop

Commander: Mucha.

1st Regiment of Samogotian Volunteer Cavalry

Commander: Maj.Gen. Jan Nagórski.

2nd Regiment of the Duchy of Samogotian Cavalry

Commander: Col. Poniatowski

Lidzki Volunteer Horse Regiment

Commander: Marcin Paszkowski
Battles: Maciejowice 10 Oct, Praga 4 Nov.

Volunteer Cavalry of Samogitia

Commander: Przeciszewski
Skirmish: Poszołoti 10 July.

Kobryń Cavalry

Commander: Maj. Gen. Kazimierz Ruszczyc.
Battles and Skirmishes: Słonim 3 Aug, Kobryń 15 Sept.

Prince Kazimierz Saphieha's Horse Regiment

Commander: Sopoćko
Formed in August.

The Cavalry Corps of Maj. Gen. Schaata

The Grodno Mounted Rifles

Commander: Lt. Col. Sochacki

Szawle Volunteers

Commanders: Maj. Gen. Stetkiewicz.
Skirmish: Zagre 9 June.

Rosieńsca Uhlans

Commander: Maj. Gen. Janusz Tyszkiewicz
Skirmishes: Zagre 9 June.

Preński's Cavalry

Commander: Col. Ułan.

Wilno Volunteers

Skirmish: Oszmiana 8 June

Army of the Targowica Confederation 1792 – 1793

National Cavalry Brigade of Hussars under the Command of the Commander of Kiev

Formed in June 1792 by the Targowice Confederation and was later incorporated into the Russian Army under the name Bohski Regiment in June 1793.
Garrisoned: Krasne, Czerkasy
Chief: Borzęcki

The uniform consisted of a crimson cap and distinctions with a blue kurtka and pants

National Cavalry Brigade "Golden Freedom" under the Command of the Commander of Podolski

Formed by the Confederation of Targowica, June 1792.
Commander: Brigadier Antoni Złotnicki, 18 June 1792

This unit was uniformed as above

National Cavalry Brigade of Hussars under the Command of the Commander of Bracławice

Formed by the Confederation of Targowica in 1792.
Garrisoned: Granów.
Commander: Brigadier Suchorzewski.

This unit was uniformed as above

Light Cavalry Regiment under the Command of Humański

Formed under the Targowica Confederation in June 1792 and was incorporated into the Russian Army under the name Winnicki Regiment in June 1793.
Garrisoned: Tulczyn, Brzostowica (III.1793).
Chief: Artillery Gen. Szczęsny Potocki
Commander: Lt. Colonel Leszczyński

Advanced Guard Regiment of the Free Confederation

Formed by the Confederation of Targowica in 1792 and in June 1793 it was incorporated into the Russian Army under the name Owrucki Regiment.

Infantry Regiment of the Free Confederation

Formed: 22 December 1792 by the Targowica Confederation with 15 companies as the 15th Infantry Regiment, disbanded in 1794
Garrisoned: Tulczyn
Chief: Adam Moszczeński
Commander: Col. Dzierżanowski.

The Targowica troops are depicted in dark blue kurtkas and pants. The headgear was a navy blue konfederatka with a lower white area and black band with a white plume.

Units of the Polish-Lithuanian Commonwealth in Battles and Skirmishes

Abbreviations

GDL – Grand Duchy of Lithuania   CNCB – Crown National Cavalry Brigade
GDNCB – Grand Duchy Lithuania National Cavalry Brigade
Adv Gd – Advanced Guard Regiment

The War of Polish Succession

4th Reg GDL Adv Gd
5th Reg GDL Adv Gd

The Seven Years War (1756 – 1763)

4th GDL Adv Gd
5th GDL Adv Gd

Ukrainian Uprising 1767

Crown Dismt Dragoon Reg

Confederation of the Bar

Grand Hetman Janissaries   Guard Crown Cavalry Reg
1st Reg King's Lancers   Crown Dismt Dragoon Reg
Horse Guards Regiment GDL

Bydgoszcz 1768
2nd Crown Inf

Chodzież 1768
2nd Crown Inf

Kościan, 1768
2nd Crown Inf

Starogród, 1768
2nd Crown Inf

Piotrków, 1768

1st Crown Inf.
2nd Crown Inf

Skrzynno, 9 April 1769

1st Crown Inf.
2nd Crown Inf

Zbąszyn

1st Crown Inf.

1792

Swisłocz
11th Crown Inf

Serby 22 May
6th CNCB   7th CNCB

Cerkinówka 22 May
7th CNCB

Opsa 22 May
1st Reg Adv Gd GDL

Mórafa 26 May
7th CNCB

Świerzeń 10 June
1st GDNCB   4th Reg GDL Adv Gd

Motowiłówka 11 June
5th CNCB   8th CNCB

Burakowski's Tavern 11 June
1st Reg of the Queen's Adv Gd

Nowa Sieniawka 11 June
6th CNCB

Mir 11 June
1st Reg of Infantry GDL   2nd Reg of Infantry GDL   4th Reg of Infantry GDL
5th Reg of Infantry GDL   6th Reg of Infantry GDL   8th Reg of Infantry GDL
1st GDNCB   2nd GDNCB   4th Reg GDL Adv Gd

Raczki 12 June
1st Reg Queen's Adv Gd

Wiszniopol 14 June
8th CNCB   5th Reg Adv Gd

Zasław
1st Crown Inf.   12th Crown Inf   8th CNCB

Boruszkowce 15 June
1st Crown Inf.   5th Crown Inf   10th Crown Inf
12th Crown Inf   13th Crown Inf   14th Crown Inf
5th CNCB   8th CNCB   1st Reg Queen's Adv Gd
5th Reg of the Crown Adv Gd

Zieleńce 17 June
1st Crown Inf.   3rd Crown Inf   4th Crown Inf
5th Crown Inf   6th Crown Inf   7th Crown Inf
9th Crown Inf   12th Crown Inf   13th Crown Inf
14th Crown Inf
2nd CNCB   3rd CNCB   5th CNCB
6th CNCB   7th CNCB   8th CNCB
1st Reg Queen's Adv Gd   2nd Reg Adv Gd   3rd Reg Adv Gd
5th Reg Adv Gd

Zelwa 4 July
11th Crown Inf
8th Reg GDL   4th Reg DGL

Izabelin 5 July
11th Crown Inf
4th Reg of Adv Gd   4th Reg GDL Adv Gd

Dubienka 7 & 8 July
3rd Crown Inf   4th Crown Inf
2nd CNCB

Włodzimierz 7 July
5th Crown Inf   9th Crown Inf   12th Crown Inf
1st Reg Queen's Adv Gd   2nd Reg of Adv Gd

Mścibów 10 July
4th Reg Adv Gd   1st Reg GDL Adv Gd   4th Reg GDL Adv Gd

Załuże 11 July
8th Reg of Inf GDL

Opalin 13 July
6th Crown Inf

Wojszki 14 July
1st Reg GDL Adv Gd

Dubienka 18 July

1st Crown Inf.	3rd Crown Inf	5th Crown Inf
12th Crown Inf	13th Crown Inf	
2nd CNCB	5th CNCB	7th CNCB
1st Reg Queen's Adv Gd	3rd Reg Adv Gd	2nd GDL NCB
2nd Reg of Loyal Cossacks of Poniatowski		

Bereżce 18 July

13th Crown Inf	14th Crown Inf
6th CNCB	

Piaski
11th Crown Inf

Szreńsk
1st CNCB

Wyszogród
1st CNCB

Łowicz
1st CNCB

Stara Rawa
1st CNCB

Rawa
1st CNCB

Breść 23 July

2nd Reg Inf GDL
7th Reg Inf GDL
4th Reg GDL Adv Gd

5th Reg Inf GDL
8th Reg Inf GDL

6th Reg Inf GDL

Granne 24 July

2nd Crown Inf
4th CNCB

11th Crown Inf

3rd Reg Inf GDL

Krzemień 24 July

11th Crown Inf

Markuszów 26 July

6th CNCB

Widawa

Horse Guards Reg GDL

Johaniszkiele (Joniŝkelis)

1st GDNCB

Zelwa 4 Aug.

3rd Reg GDL Adv Gd

1794

Inowłódź 21 Mar
1st CBNC

Kozubowo 25 Mar
4th CBNC

Opatów 29 Mar
4th CBNC

Końskie 1 Apr
1st CBNC

Racławice 4 Apr

2nd Crown Inf	3rd Crown Inf	6th Crown Inf
1st Krakow Grenadiers	2nd CBNC	
1st CBNC	4th CBNC	4th Reg Adv Gd

Warsaw Uprising 17 - 19 April

5th Crown Inf	10th Crown Inf	11th Crown Inf
Hun Co. Great Marshal Crown	Crown Treasury Militia	
Guard Crown Cavalry Reg	1st Reg King's Lancers	

Wilno 22/23 Apr

4th Reg Inf. GDL	7th Reg Inf. GDL

Nowy Dwór 26 April
1st Reg King's Lancers

Stanisławów 26 Apr
3rd CBNC

Białorękawy 30 April
7th CNCB

Stary Konstantynów 1 May
7th CNCB

Nowe – Miasto 3 May
11th Crown Inf

Szczucin 13 May
1st GDNCB

Poniewież 20 May
1st GDNCB

Rosławice 22 May
Cavalry detachment of horse pikemen   Mazurzian Horse

Mikołajów 23 May
2nd GDNCB

Serocka 29 May
5th Crown Inf   Rifle Battalion of Kalice

Szemberk 3 June
Kowieński's Lt Inf Battalion

Szczekociny 6 June
1st Crown Inf	2nd Crown Inf	3rd Crown Inf
4th Crown Inf	6th Crown Inf	7th Crown Inf
9th Crown Inf	13th Crown Inf	1st Krakow Grenadiers
Sandomierz Grenadiers		
1st CBNC	2nd CBNC	4th CBNC
1st Reg Queen's Adv Gd	4th Reg Adv Gd	5th Reg Adv Gd

Chełm 8 June
5th Crown Inf	9th Crown Inf	11th Crown Inf
18th Crown Inf		
3rd CNCB	7th CNCB	3rd Reg Adv Gd
4th Reg Adv Gd	Lt. Sierpiński's free Cossacks	Sokoł's Cavalry detachment

Oszmiana 8 June
Wilno Volunteers

Zagre 9 June
Szawle Volunteers   Rosieńsca Uhlans

Radziwiliszki 12 June
Kowieński's Light Infantry Battalion

Szkudy 12 July
1st GDNCB

Promnika 14 June
Militia of Krakow   1rst Krakow Grenadiers

Lipow Pola, 15 June
Troops of Radom

Wołożyn 15 June
Free Light Infantry Ogiński

Warsaw, 17 June
1st Reg Queen's Adv Gd   5th Reg Adv Gd

Iwienic 19 June
Free Light Infantry Ogiński   Wilno Cavalry

Zagóra 22 June
Szawelscy Riflemen

Soły 25 June
5th Reg Inf GDL   7th Reg Inf GDL
8th Reg Inf GDL   Light Infantry Battalion Grabiński

Końskie 26 June
1st CBNC

Kurów
11th Crown Inf

Uściług 28 June
3rd CBNC   3rd Reg Adv Gd

Starczyska 29 June
1st CNCB

Gołchów 29 June
3rd CNCB   Sokoł's Cavalry detachment

Kumelsk 1 July
Troops of Bielski

Lachów 1 July
Troops of Bielski

Lachowa 1 July
Light Infantry from Bielski

Sochaczew 1 & 4 July
8th CNCB

Stawiski 3 July
18th Crown Inf   Troops of Bielski   Bielsk pikemen

Kolno 7 July
Vol. Horse Reg Col. Kwaśniewski.

Rajgrod 7 July
Troops of Bielski

Włodzimierz 7 July
7th CNCB

Gołków 9 July
7th Crown Inf   9th Crown Inf   11th Crown Inf
1st CNCB   7th CNCB   2nd GD NCB

Błonie 9 July
8th CNCB   5th Reg Adv Gd

Raszyn 10 July
7th Crown Inf   9th Crown Inf
7th CNCB

Poszołoty 10 July
Scythemen of Wiłkomirsca

Vol Cav of Samogatia

Bereże 18 July
7th CNCB

Wilna 19 and 20 July
Wilno Cavalry

Wola 27 July
9th Crown Inf

1st Krakow Grenadiers

7th CNCB

2nd GD NCB

Powązki 28 July
Crown Foot Guards

1st Crown Inf

8th CNCB

3rd Reg Adv Gd

Sałaty 29 July
1st Reg Inf GDL

6th Reg Inf GDL   Wileńsciand Upitsci Lt. Inf

Czerniaków 31 July
1st CNCB

Słonim 1-3 Aug
5th Crown Inf

Warsaw Mun. Vol Battalion

Guard Crown Cav Reg

1st Reg King's Lancers   Kobryń Cavalry

Around Warsaw Aug
2nd Crown Inf

6th Crown Inf   11th Crown Inf

13th Crown Inf

19th Crown Inf   20th Crown Inf

Hung. Com. Great Marshal Crown

Cap. Ludwik Dembowski's Rifles

1st Krakow Grenadiers

1st CNCB

2nd CNCB   3rd CNCB

4th CNCB

7th CNCB   8th CNCB

1st Reg Queen's Adv Gd

3rd Reg Adv Gd   Mazurzian Horse

2nd GDNCB

Cybulice 8 Aug
Mazurzian Horse

Wilno 10 Aug.
2nd GDNCB

Wilno 11 Aug.

1st Reg Inf GDL	3rd Reg Inf GDL
3rd GDNCB	6th Reg GDL Adv Gd

Witkowice 13 Aug

13th Crown Inf	3rd CNCB

Górce, 14 Aug

Crown Foot Guards	9th Crown Inf
Rifle Bat. Lt. Col. F. Ksawery Rymkiewicz	
8th CNCB	

Zegrze, 18 Aug

Crown Foot Guards	15th Crown Inf	16th Crown Inf
1st Reg King's Lancers		

Lachy 19 Aug
1st CNCB

Karczma
Crown Foot Guards

Zbarz
2nd CNCB

Ostrołęka 19 August

15th Crown Inf	Łomżyńa Rifles - Gen. Wiszowata

Rakowiec 17 & 18 Aug

13th Crown Inf	1st Krakow Grenadiers
2nd CNCB	

Szczęśliwice 17 & 18 Aug

2nd Crown Inf	Maj. Biegański's Rifles
1st Reg Queen's Adv Gd	

Powązki 18 Aug
13th Crown Inf

| 7th CNCB | 8th CNCB | 3rd Reg Adv Gd |

Ryka 23 August
Troops of Garwołińa

Swedish Battery 25 Aug
2nd GDNCB

Nieporęt 25 Aug
Januszkiewicz's Rifles

Narwią 25 Aug
Troops of Nurska

Grabowo 25 Aug
Łomżyńa Rifles - Gen. Wiszowata

Marymont 26 Aug.

| 9th Crown Inf | 19th Crown Inf |

Wola 26 Aug
| 9th Crown Inf | 11th Crown Inf |

Cap. Ludwik Dembowski's Rifles

Wawrzyszew 27 Aug
| 4th Crown Inf | 9th Crown Inf | 13th Crown Inf |

Rifle Bat. Lt. Col. F. Ksawery Rymkiewicz   Riflemen of Starzeński
7th CNCB

Dęblina 27 Aug
"3rd Regiment of Horse"

Wola 28 Aug
| 11th Crown Inf | Troops of Mielnick |

Powązki 28 Aug
| Col. Piotrowski's Cav detachment | 2nd GDNCB |

Góra 28 Aug
"3rd Regiment of Horse"

Tokary and Witkowice 28 Aug
8th CNCB

Wisła 29 Aug
"3rd Regiment of Horse"

Welański
Crown Foot Guards

Skalmierz
4th Reg Adv Gd

Czerniaków 31 July
5th Reg Adv Gd

Bielany 1 Sept
4th Crown Inf   9th Crown Inf

Błonie 9 Sept
2nd GDNCB

Troszczynem 14 Sept
Troops of Nurska

Kobryń 15 Sept
Kobryń Cavalry

Sielec 17 Sept
4th CNCB

Krupczyce 17 Sept.
Crown Foot Guards
5th Crown Inf   15th Crown Inf   18th Crown Inf
19th Crown Inf   Warsaw Mun Vol Batl   Bresc-Litowsk Battalion
Guard Crown Cavalry Regiment
4th Reg Adv Gd   5th Reg Adv Gd   1st Reg King's Lancers
3rd Reg Adv Gd GDL   The Grodzieński Cav Reg

Rzewnie 18 Sept
4th CNCB

Brześć 19 Sept
Crown Foot Guards

15th Crown Inf	18th Crown Inf	19th Crown Inf

Warsaw Mun Vol Battalion
Guard Crown Cavalry Reg

4th Reg Adv Gd	5th Reg Adv Gd	1st Reg King's Lancers
1st GDNCB	3rd Reg Adv Gd	Grodzieński Cav Reg

Terespol 19 Sept
18th Crown Inf

Kadniewek
4th CNCB

Gzowo
4th CNCB

Magnuszew
8th Reg Av Gd GDL

Strzyże 20
4th CNCB

Nadarzyn 22 Sept
Col. Toliński's Cav detachment

Nowogród 22 Sept.
Troops from Bielski

Strzyże 24 Sept

3rd CNCB	4th CNCB	1st Reg Queen's Adv Gd

Biała 27 Sept

11th Crown Inf	5th Reg Adv Gd

Żuków and Kamionna 4 Oct
8th CNCB

Dereczyn
4th Reg Adv Gd GDL

Bzurą River 6 Oct
8th CNCB

Maciejowice 10 Oct
Crown Foot Guards

2nd Crown Inf	3rd Crown Inf	5th Crown Inf
10th Crown Inf	11th Crown Inf	15th Crown Inf
16th Crown Inf	18th Crown Inf	1st Krakow Grenadiers

Warsaw Mun Vol Battalion
Guard Crown Cavalry Regiment

3rd CNCB	5th Reg Adv Gd	1st Reg King's Lancers
Starozakonna Lt Cav Reg	2nd GDNCB	3rd Reg Adv Gd GDL
4th Reg Adv Gd GDL	Grodzieński Cav Reg	Lidzki Vol Horse Reg

Praga 4 Nov
Crown Foot Guards

3rd Crown Inf	4th Crown Inf	5th Crown Inf
6th Crown Inf	15th Crown Inf	16th Crown Inf
Maj. Biegański's Rifles	1st Krakow Grenadiers	Warsaw Mun Vol Battalion
Riflemen of Col. Ossowski	Troops of Drohicki	1st Reg Queen's Adv Gd
1st Reg King's Lancers	Starozakonna Lt Cav Reg	Vol Reg Col. Kwaśniewski.
Col. Toliński's Cav detachment	3rd Reg Inf GDL	4th Reg Inf GDL
5th Reg Inf GDL	7th Reg Inf GDL	Lt Inf Battalion Grabiński
Scythemen of Wiłkomirsca	Grodno Lt Inf I	Grodno Lt Inf II
Wolan Lt Inf	Insur. Militia Wołkowyski,	
2nd GDNCB	2nd Reg Adv Gd GDL	3rd Reg Adv Gd GDL
4th Reg Adv Gd	5th Reg Adv Gd	Lidzki Vol Horse Reg

Radoszyce 18 Nov
2nd Crown Inf

Hetmen of the Polish - Lithanian Commonwealth

Polish Grand Hetman

1706 – 1726	Adam Mikołaj Sieniawski
1726 – 1728	Stainsław Mateusz Rzewuski
1728 – 1735	Vacant
1735 – 1751	Józef Potocki
1752 – 1771	Jan Klemens Branicki
1773 – 1773	Wacław Rzewuski
1774 – 1793	Franciszek Ksawery Branicki
1793 – 1794	Piotr Ożarowski

Polish Field Hetman

1706 – 1726	Stainsław Mateusz Rzewuski
1726 – 1728	Stanisław Chomętowski
1728 – 1736	Vacant
1736 – 1752	Jan Klemens Branicki
1752 – 1773	Wacław Rzewuski
1774 – 1774	Franciszek Ksawery Branicki
1774 – 1794	Seweryn Rzewuski

Lithuanian Grand Hetman

1707 – 1708	Jan Kazimierz Sapieha the Younger
1708 – 1709	Jan Kazimierz Sapieha the Eldar
1709 – 1709	Gregorz Antoni Ogiński
1709 – 1730	Ludwik Pociej
1735 – 1744	Michał Serwacy Wisniowiecki
1744 – 1762	Michał Kazimierz Radziwiłł
1762 – 1768	Michał Józef Massalski
1769 – 1793	Michał Kazimierz Oginski
1793 – 1794	Szymon Marcin Kossakowski

Lithuanian Field Hetman

1707 – 1709	Michał Serwacy Wisniowiecki
1709 – 1728	Stanisław Ernest Denoff
1735 – 1742	Michał Kazimierz Radziwiłł
1742 – 1762	Michał Józef Massalski
1762 – 1775	Aleksander Michał Sapieha
1775 – 1780	Józef Sosnowski
1780 – 1791	Ludwik Tyszkiewicz
1792 – 1793	Szymon Marcin Kossakowski
1793 – 1794	Józef Zabiello

Bibliography

Anusiewicz, Marion (ed) & Gembarzewski, Zolnierz polski od 1697 do 1794 roku (Wydawnictwo Ministerstwa Obrony Narodowej; Warszawa, 1963)

www.Arsenal.org.pl., *Rekonstrukcja mundura towarzysza Kawalerii Narodowej Koronnej z lat 1791 – 1794* (2001)

www.Arsenal.org.pl., *Brygada I Kawalerii narodowej* (2009)

www.Arsenal.org.pl., *Korpus artilleria Oboyga narodowi* 1792 (2009)

Ciesielski, Tomasz, *Armia Koronna w czasach Augusta III.* (Instytut Historii Uniwersytetu Opolskiego: Warsawa, 2009)

Cranz, Philip, *The Army of the Grand Duchy of Warsaw: Vol III Infantry* (Uniformology: Weatherford, 2008)

Czop, Jan, Barwa *Wojska Rzeczypospolitej Obojga narodów w XVIII wieku* (Libra: Rzeszow, 2009)

Davies, Norman, *God's Playgorund: A History of Poland, Vols I, II* (Columbia University Press: New York, 1982)

Gerbarzewski, Bronisław, *Rodowody Pułkow Polskich I Oddziałow Rownorzednych od 1717 do r 1831. Nakladem* (Tow Wiedzy Wojskowej: Warszawa, 1925)

Haiman, Miecislaus, *Kosciuszko: Leader in Exile* (Kosciuszko Foundation: New York, 1977)

Jedruch, Jacek, *Constitutions, Elections and Legislatures of Poland, 1493 – 1993: A Guide to their History* (EJJ Books: New York, 1998)

Kannik, Preben, *Military Uniforms of the World in Color* (MacMillian Publishing Co, Inc.: New York, 1962)

Kaplan, Herbert H., *The First Partition of Poland* (Columbia University Press: New York, 1962)

Knotel, Richard, Knotel, Herbert & Sieg, Herbert, *Uniforms of the World* (Charles Scribner & Son: New York, 1980)

Kom. Eduk. Narod. *Regulamen Exercerunku dla Regimentow Konnych Gwardyi* (Drukarni Nadworney: Warszawa, 1786)

Kommissya Woyskowa, Przepis Musztry dla Regimentow Pieszych Woyska Koronnego y W.X. Litewskiego (Warszawa, 1790)

Korbal, Rafat, *Dzieje Wojska Polskiego* (Wydawnictwo Podsiedlik-Raniowski I Spolka: Poznan,

1990)

Lubicz-Pachonski, Jan, *Bitwa pod Racławicami* (Panstwowe Wydawnictwo Naukowe: Warszawa, 1984)

Maslowski, Maciej, *Juliusz Kossak* (Wydawnictwa Artystyczne I Filmowe: Warszawa, 1982)

Nowak, Jan & Wimmer, Jan, *Historia Oreza Polskiego 963 - 1795* (Wiedza Powszechna: Warszawa, 1981)

Pachonski, Jan, *General Jan Henryk Dąbrowski 1755 – 1818* (Wydawnictwo Ministerstwa Obrony Narodowej: Warszawa, 1981)

Pachonski, Jan, *Legiony Polskie: Prawda I Legenda 1794 – 1807* (Wydawnictwo Ministerstwa Obrany Narodowej: Warszawa, 1979)

Pogonowski, Iwo Cyprian, *Poland: A Historical Atlas* (Hippocrene Books, Inc: New York, 1987)

Poniatowski, Jan, *Wojsko Kosciuszkowskie Na Plotnie Panoramy Raclawickie* (Ossolineum: Wroclaw, 1990)

Ratajczyk, Leonard & Jerszy Teodorczyk, *Wojsko Powstania Kosciuszkowskiego* (Wydawnictwo Ministerstwa Obrony Narodowej: Warszawa, 1987)

Ratajczyk, Leonard, *Wojsko I obronnosc Rzeczypospolitej 1788 – 1792* (Wydawnictwo Ministeria Obrony Narodowej: Warszawa, 1975)

Rymkiewicz, Jarosław Marek, *The Hangings* (Transl. Mateusz Julecki, Winged Hussar publishing, LLC: Pt Pleasant, 2022)

Skowronek, Jerzy, *Ksiaze Józef Poniatowski* (Ossonlineum: Wrocław, 1984)

Smolinski, Aleksander, *Munur I Barwy artylerii polskiej w XVIII I XIX wieku* (Wydawnictwo Naukowe Uniwersytetu Mikołaja Koperniki: Torun, 2010)

Storozynski, Alex, *The Peasant Prince* (St Martins Press: New York, 2009)

Twardowski, Bolesław, *Wojsko Polskie Kosciuszko w roku 1794* (Nakladem Ksiegarni Katolickiej: Poznan, 1894)

Wallis, Mieczylaw, *Canaletto Malarz Warszawy*, (Wydawnictwa Artystyczne I Filmowe: Warszawa, 1983)

Zamoyski, Adam, *Poland: A History* (Harper Press: London, 2009)

Zamoyski, Adam, *The Last king of Poland*, (Cape: London, 1992)

Ziejka, Franciszek, *Panorama Racławicka*, (Krajowa Agencja Wydawnicza: Krakow, 1984)

Zygulski, Zdzisław & Wielecki, Henryk, *Polski mundur Wojskowy* (Krajowa Agencja Wydawnicza w Krakowie: Krakow, 1988)

Index

Look for more books from Winged Hussar Publishing, LLC – E-books, paperbacks and Limited-Edition hardcovers. The best in history, science fiction and fantasy at:

https://www. wingedhussarpublishing.com

https://www.whpsupplyroom.com

or follow us on Facebook at:

Winged Hussar Publishing LLC

Or on twitter at:

WingHusPubLLC

For information and upcoming publications

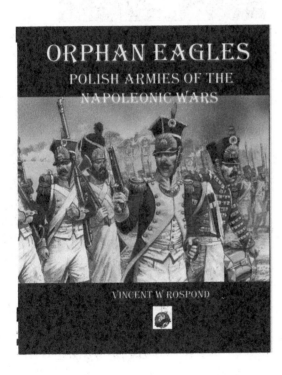

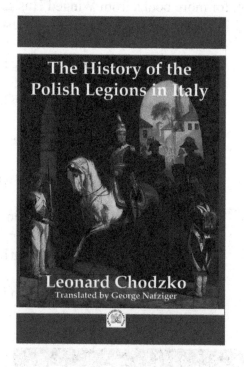

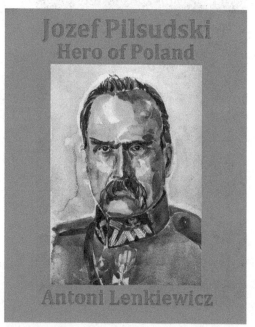

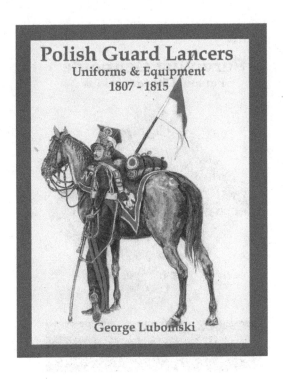

Polish Guard Lancers
Uniforms & Equipment
1807 - 1815

George Lubomski

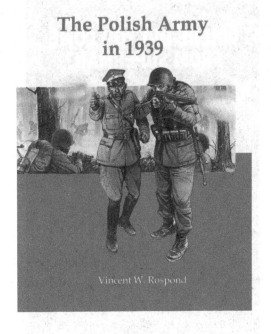

**The Polish Army
in 1939**

Vincent W. Rospond

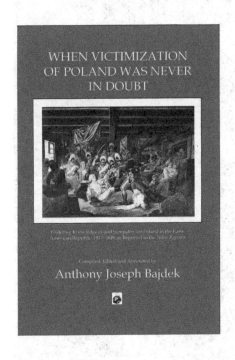

WHEN VICTIMIZATION
OF POLAND WAS NEVER
IN DOUBT

Fostering Knowledge and Sympathy for Poland in the Early
American Republic, 1811-1849, as Reported in the Niles' Register

Compiled, Edited and Annotated by
Anthony Joseph Bajdek

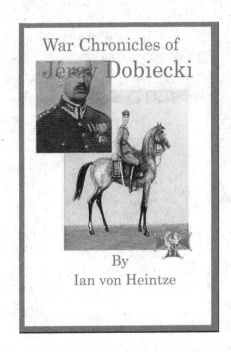

War Chronicles of
Jerzy Dobiecki

By
Ian von Heintze

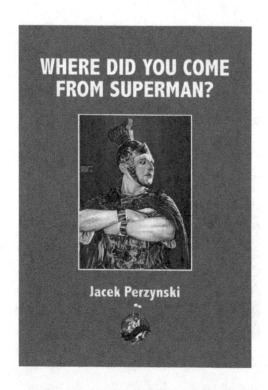

WHERE DID YOU COME FROM SUPERMAN?

Jacek Perzynski

Surviving Genocide
Personal Recollections

By
Donna Chmara

PAN TADEUSZ
OR THE LAST FORAY IN LITHUANIA
ADAM MICKIEWICZ

TRANSLATED BY
CHRISTOPHER ADAM ZAKRZEWSKI

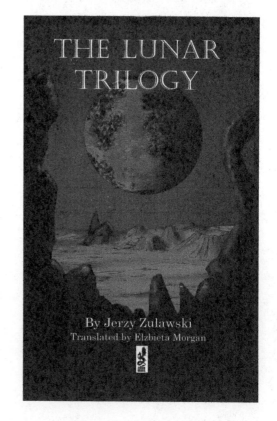

THE LUNAR TRILOGY

By Jerzy Zulawski
Translated by Elzbieta Morgan

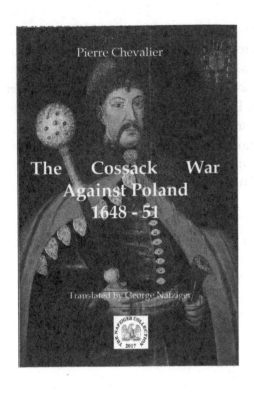

Pierre Chevalier

The Cossack War Against Poland 1648 - 51

Translated by George Nafziger

Fire on the Steppes
Three Accounts of the War Against the Turks
1588 - 1683

Translated by George Nafziger

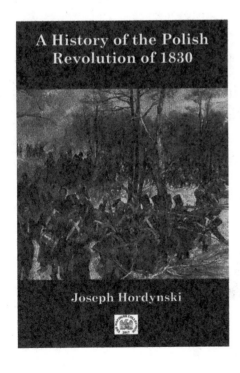

A History of the Polish Revolution of 1830

Joseph Hordynski

God's Eye
Aerial Photography and the Katyn Forest Massacre

Frank Fox

Bronisław Gembarzewski (May 30, 1872 - December 11, 1941) - a colonel of sappers in the Polish Army, battle painter, military historian, museologist, longtime director of the National Museum and the Military Museum in Warsaw. He studied painting at the Academy of Fine Arts in St. Petersburg [1] (1892–1894) and at the Conservatoire national des arts et métiers in Paris (1895–1896). He was called into the Imperial Russian Army in 1914 where he served as a captain of the engineers. From 1916 to 1936 he was the director of the National Museum in Warsaw, and from 1920 the director of the Military Museum in Warsaw. After the outbreak of World War II, he was briefly imprisoned in Pawiak Prison, and after his release, he took part in the rescue of the monuments of the Military Museum in Warsaw. He is buried at the Powązki Cemetery in Warsaw.

Vincent Rospond is a historian specializing in Polish history

Winged Hussar Publishing, LLC
Point Pleasant, NJ